WIZARDING WORLDS

Inside the Harry Potter Theme Parks, Exhibitions, and Studio Tours

WILLIAM SILVESTER

Theme Park Press
The Happiest Books on Earth
www.ThemeParkPress.com

© 2017 William Silvester

No part of this publication may be reproduced, distributed, or transmitted in any form or by any means, including photocopying, recording, or other electronic or mechanical methods, without the prior written permission of the publisher, except for brief quotations embodied in critical reviews and certain other non-commercial uses permitted by copyright law.

Although every precaution has been taken to verify the accuracy of the information contained herein, no responsibility is assumed for any errors or omissions, and no liability is assumed for damages that may result from the use of this information.

This book is not authorized, approved, licensed or endorsed by J. K. Rowling, her publishers, or Warner Bros. Entertainment Inc. Harry Potter characters, names and related indicia are trademarks of and © Warner Bros. Entertainment Inc. Harry Potter Publishing Rights © JKR.

The views expressed in this book are those of the author and do not necessarily reflect the views of Theme Park Press.

Theme Park Press publishes its books in a variety of print and electronic formats. Some content that appears in one format may not appear in another.

Editor: Bob McLain
Layout: Artisanal Text

ISBN 978-1-68390-090-0
Printed in the United States of America

Theme Park Press | www.ThemeParkPress.com
Address queries to bob@themeparkpress.com

CONTENTS

CHAPTER 1
In the Beginning

CHAPTER 2
Harry Potter Movie Magic Experience

CHAPTER 3
Harry Potter: The Exhibition

CHAPTER 4
Building a Wizarding World

CHAPTER 5
Inside the Wizarding World—Hogsmeade

CHAPTER 6
Inside the Wizarding World—Diagon Alley

CHAPTER 7
Warner Bros. Studio Tours Leavesden

CHAPTER 8
Inside the Wizarding World—Japan

CHAPTER 9
Harry Potter in Hollywood

CHAPTER 10
The Rest of the Wizarding World

Bibliography
About the Author
About Theme Park Press

CHAPTER ONE
IN THE BEGINNING

Harry Potter was conceived in the fertile mind of Joanne Rowling on a train traveling from Manchester to London in the summer of 1990. The train had stopped for some mechanical problem and Rowling was content to sit and stare out the window letting her mind wander as she watched cows in a nearby field. As she later told an interviewer: "All of a sudden the idea for Harry just appeared in my mind's eye. I can't tell you why or what triggered it. But I saw the idea of Harry and the wizard school very plainly. I have never been so excited about an idea."

Having neither pen, pencil, nor paper handy for jotting down notes, Rowling sat quietly and allowed her imagination to take her to this school she saw in her mind. She traversed its corridors, imaged and named some of the teachers, ghosts, and the groundskeeper. She placed the school, a castle she named Hogwarts, in the wild Scottish Highlands and decided students would get to it in a train, a magical train that regular people could not see.

Once she arrived home, she wrote down everything she dreamed about on the train and expanded on those ideas to flesh out her characters and the plot of what would become *Harry Potter and the Philosopher's Stone*.

Chipping Sodbury General Hospital in Yate, Gloucestershire, England, was the birthplace of Joanne Rowling on July 31, 1965. Her parents, Peter and Ann Rowling, and later a sister, Diane, moved several times in her early years from Yate to Winterbourne to Tutshill. Her greatest love was writing and telling stories and though quiet and reserved she graduated from school as Head Girl.

Furthering her education at Exeter University she studied French and lived in Paris for a year. Later she was employed at Amnesty International and held a variety of secretarial jobs. None of these held any great interest for her and she continued to write whenever an opportunity arose.

Her twenty-sixth year was one of emotional turmoil. Her mother had been diagnosed with multiple sclerosis, her relationship with her boyfriend was not going well, and she was out of work. Harry Potter was the only real joy in her life. She began creating the wizarding world in her every spare minute.

But dreams did not put food on the table nor pay the rent, so Rowling took a job teaching English as a second language in Oporto, Portugal, in September 1990. She found a comfortable apartment, discovered that she enjoyed her job, and settled into a routine of teaching and writing. In December, her mother died and the loss was reflected in her writing about the orphaned Harry Potter.

Romance now entered her life in the form of TV journalist Jorge Arantes. After her marriage to Arantes, and just before her twenty-eighth birthday, she gave birth to her daughter, Jessica. By this time, she had completed the first three chapters of *Harry Potter and the Philosopher's Stone*, and had written the rest of the book in rough draft form.

Unfortunately, her marriage did not work out. She separated from her husband and returned to Britain with her daughter. Her sister, Diane, lived in Edinburgh, Scotland, and it was here that Rowling continued her writing while looking for another job. Whenever she could, Rowling wheeled her baby to Nicolson's Café, owned by her brother-in-law, and spent the hours writing while the child slept. Finally, after five years of work, she finished the manuscript.

The book was rejected on her first attempts to market it, but literary agent Christopher Little saw the potential and so did Bloomsbury Press who paid her a $4,000 advance in October 1996. A few months later Rowling was awarded a Scottish Arts Council grant that enabled her to buy a computer and write *Harry Potter and the Chamber of Secrets*. Her biggest break came in April of the same year when Scholastic Books bid $105,000 for the American rights to *Harry Potter and the*

IN THE BEGINNING

Philosopher's Stone (changing the name to *Harry Potter and the Sorcerer's Stone*). Now she could quit her job and become a full-time writer.

Harry Potter and the Philosopher's Stone was published in Britain in late June 1997 with an initial print run of only 500 books. Rowling was asked to use her initials instead of her name for fear that boys would not want to read a book written by a woman. She adopted her grandmother's name, Kathleen, as a second name, and the book was published as written by J.K. Rowling.

It was a huge success and garnered several awards. When the time came to publish the second book in the series, *Harry Potter and the Chamber of Secrets,* the print run was increased to 10,000. Meanwhile, the first book was printed in the United States with a run of 50,000 copies, but American readers had to resort to buying book two online as *Harry Potter and the Chamber of Secrets* did not come out in the US until the summer of 1999.

Now Joanne Rowling had two books at the top of the best seller lists and they were soon to be joined by a third, *Harry Potter and the Prisoner of Azkaban.* So popular were the books that when Rowling made a three-week book tour of the US the venues were mobbed by excited fans.

The year 2000 was to be a particularly exciting one for Potterdom as it was announced that Warner Bros. had signed a contract to make the Harry Potter books into films. With the films would be the beginning of Harry Potter merchandising. In July of the same year, the fourth book in the series, *Harry Potter and the Goblet of Fire*, was published simultaneously in the UK and US with a combined first run of 5 million books. In 2001 the Harry Potter Movie Magic Experience opened in Warner Bros. Movie World in Australia, the first time actual props from the Harry Potter films were exhibited.

Potter fans were now in for a long wait as Rowling worked on the fifth book that would not be released until 2003. In the meantime, two of the schoolbooks used at Hogwarts, *Quidditch Through the Ages* and *Fantastic Beasts and Where to Find Them*, were published to benefit the British charity Comic Relief. The first of the Harry Potter films was also released, setting record grosses on both sides of the Atlantic. Rowling ended the year on a happy personal note when she married anesthesiologist Neil Murray.

Harry Potter and the Chamber of Secrets was released on film in November 2002, again setting box office records. The long wait for book five was finally over in mid-2003 when *Harry Potter and the Order of the Phoenix*, the longest in the series, was finally published. Rowling and her husand became the proud parents of her second child, David.

Harry Potter and the Prisoner of Azkaban opened in theaters in May 2004 with a new director and a different actor as Professor Dumbledore. The following year, Rowling gave birth to her third child, Mackenzie, and in July the sixth book, *Harry Potter and the Half-Blood Prince*, was released followed in November by the film version of *Harry Potter and the Goblet of Fire*.

Throughout 2006, Rowling was hard at work raising her children, supporting her charities, and finishing the last of the Harry Potter series. *Harry Potter and the Deathly Hallows* was completed at Edinburgh's Balmoral Hotel in January 2007 and published in July. Ten days previous, the release of *Harry Potter and the Order of the Phoenix* in theaters had broken all records for Harry Potter opening days.

Back in North America again, Rowling began her "Open Book Tour" in Los Angeles and traveled to New York and Toronto. About this time she penned seven copies of *The Tales of Beedle the Bard* and sold one at auction for charity. A documentary film, *J. K. Rowling, A Year in the Life*, aired on British television at the end of the year.

The Tales of Beedle the Bard was published for general distribution in 2008 at a children's tea party hosted by Rowling. Production began on *Harry Potter and the Half-Blood Prince* for release in 2009 and Harry Potter: The Exhibition began touring the world. Earlier in the year, Rowling had the title Knight of the Legion of Honour bestowed upon her by the French president. In response, she apologized for giving her greatest villain, Voldemort, a French name.

Harry Potter and the Deathly Hallows was released in two parts in 2010 and 2011. The Wizarding World of Harry Potter—Hogsmeade opened in Universal Studios Orlando in

2010 and expanded to include Diagon Alley and the Hogwarts Express in 2014. Wizarding World of Harry Potter opened in Universal Studios Japan a few weeks later. Warner Bros. Studio Tour London—The Making of Harry Potter opened at Leavesden Studio in England, expanding on what had begun in Australia in 2001. Universal Studios Hollywood opened their version of Wizarding World of Harry Potter in 2016 accompanied by Warner Bros. Studio Tour Hollywood—Harry Potter and Fantastic Beasts.

The first part of what will eventually be five films based on *Fantastic Beasts and Where to Find Them* was released in December 2016 and was Rowling's first screenplay. Also in 2016 was the release of the stage play *Harry Potter and the Cursed Child* written by British playwright Jack Thorne and based on an original story by Rowling, Thorne, and John Tiffany. A British Museum exhibit, Harry Potter: A History of Magic, premiered in 2017.

A plethora of TV documentaries, hundreds of books about the author and her creation, and thousands of items of related merchandise evolved from the adventures of "the boy who lived."

While most of the former are interconnected, it is the history and development of the theme parks and exhibitions that will be related here. This book was not written to be a tour guide, though parts of it may be useful in that respect; rather it is a history of and a behind-the-scenes look at all that went into making the wonder and magic of the Wizarding Worlds of Harry Potter. The author has attempted to at least mention, if not go into detail describing, every shop, store, and restaurant within the Wizarding Worlds. They are listed, for the most part, in alphabetical order rather than as they would be encountered during a tour of the parks.

Several books have been written about the Wizarding World of Harry Potter, but most if not all of them deals with the Universal Orlando park exclusively. This book is about all the Wizarding World parks as well as numerous other aspects of Harry Potter exhibitions and shows.

The author presupposes that the reader has a certain degree of familiarity with Harry Potter either through the books, the films, or a combination of the two. Any attempt to explain every allusion made to the books or films within the Wizarding Worlds would require more than one book, though some effort is made to do just that. There are quite a few spoilers for those uninitiated in Potterlore, but even though some of the attraction descriptions might give away a few details, they cannot be compared to actually viewing the props and special effects.

The author also prefers to use the term "Potterphile" when referring to ardent fans as he feels the more popular "Potterhead" is verging on the derogatory and is too close to the drug-related term "pothead."

CHAPTER TWO

HARRY POTTER MOVIE MAGIC EXPERIENCE

Australia led the world in Harry Potter movie experiences. Though the island nation did not play a large part in the Harry Potter books or films, it was not unmentioned. For example, according to Kennilworthy Whisp's textbook *Quidditch Through the Ages*, Australia has its own National Stadium and a national Quidditch team, formed in the 18th century. The Australian Quidditch League is comprised of the Western Australia's Thunderlarra Thunderers and New South Wales' Woollongong (Wollongong) Warriors. These two teams dominated the league and were renowned as much for their hostility toward each other as for their speed and showmanship. Other Oceania countries also participated in the Australian league which took advantage of the wide open, remote, and largely uninhabited Australian outback to establish Quidditch pitches. The national team won the Quidditch World Cup in 1996.

The island is also the home to several magical creatures such as the speedy, sapphire blue insect known as the Billywig and a werewolf that Gilderoy Lockhart claimed to have defeated near Wagga Wagga. A breed of dragon, native to New Zealand, known as the Antipodean Opaleye has been known to migrate to Australia for more living space.

It appears that the wizarding world was aware of the existence of Australia before it was discovered by Muggles. In *Wonderbook: Book of Potions*, written by Zygmunt Budge sometime in the 1500s, the author referred to Australia as if it was well known when it fact it was not discovered by Muggles until 1606.

Seven of the eleven large magical schools around the world have been identified by name and include Hogwarts (Great Britain), Durmstrang (Northern Europe), Beauxbatons (France), Uagadou (Africa), Castelobruxo (Brazil), Ilvermorny (United States), and Mahoutokoro (Japan). There is said to a school located in Canada and another in Australia.

The most poignant mention of Australia was made in *Harry Potter and the Deathly Hallows* when Hermione Granger altered her parent's memories and sent them to Sydney to manage a sweet shop to protect them from Lord Voldemort. Living under the aliases of Wendell and Monica Wilkins, they stayed safely out of harm's way until after the Second Wizarding War when Hermione restored their memories.

In 2001, as anticipation for the film release of *Harry Potter and the Philosopher's Stone* reached fever pitch in Australia, Warner Bros. sought a way to capitalize on the excitement. They already had a theme park on the Gold Coast known as Warner Bros. Movie World, or simply, Movie World. It had opened in June 1991 and was Australia's only movie-related theme park.

The story of the Australian Warner Bros. park began in 1989 when C.V. Wood, who already had Six Flags Over Texas and Disneyland on his résumé, was hired to design a 415-acre (168 hectare) theme park in the swampland next to the Warner Bros. Roadshow Studio. He completed the task in 16 months, having based his concept on the successful parks of Universal Studios and Disney-MGM Studios at Walt Disney World. The park was officially located at Pacific Highway, Oxenford, Gold Coast, Queensland.

Queensland Premier Wayne Goss attended the official opening ceremony on June 3, 1991, and opened the park by cutting a novelty film reel alongside Clint Eastwood, Kurt Russell, Goldie Hawn, and Mel Gibson.

The initial premise of the park was to teach visitors about film making by getting them involved in behind-the-scenes magic and movie action. Opening day attractions included the Movie Studio Tour, Western Action Show, Young Einstein Gravity Homestead, Police Academy Stunt Show, and Classics & Great Gremlins Adventure. Looney Tunes Land featured a Looney Tunes River Ride and the Looney Tunes Musical Revue.

HARRY POTTER MOVIE MAGIC EXPERIENCE

In 1992 the park expanded with Batman Adventure—The Ride. A few years later the Western Action Show was replaced by the Maverick Grand Illusion Show along with the park's first roller coaster, Lethal Weapon—The Ride.

Looney Tunes Village changed to Looney Tunes Land in 1997 as several new Zamperla rides were introduced: Yosemite Sam's Railroad, Taz Hollywood Cars, Tweety and Sylvester Carousel, and Marvin the Martian's Rocket Ride. A new 3D show starring Marvin the Martian replaced Adventures in the Fourth Dimension at the Roxy Theatre.

Expansion continued in 1998 when an $18 million Wild, Wild West ride (later renamed Wild West Falls Adventure Ride) opened. The Looney Tunes Musical Revue was moved in 2000 and the Road Runner Rollercoaster constructed on its spot. At the same time, Young Einstein Gravity Homestead was shut down.

For the 10th anniversary in 2001, a number of live shows were introduced. The Maverick Show was closed as was Classics & the Great Gremlin Adventure. Batman Adventure—The Ride was redone as Batman Adventure—The Ride 2 featuring a motion simulator and new films. Soon after, the Looney Tunes Splash Zone was added to Looney Tunes Village.

Like most theme parks, Movie World had costumed characters such as Batman, Austin Powers, Scooby Doo, and assorted Looney Tunes characters wandering the park to encourage photo ops with visitors. An All-Star parade featured movie-themed floats and movie costumes along with short street shows with singing and dancing characters. Part of the theme park adjacent to Warner Bros. Roadshow Studio was designated a working studio and saw the production of several Warner Bros. films and TV shows, from *Scooby Doo* to *Ghost Ship*.

What better place to build a Harry Potter addition?

The addition was to be called the Harry Potter Movie Magic Experience and would be constructed on the site of the former Young Einstein Gravity Homestead. As a walk-through attraction, it would feature the re-creation of several sets from the Harry Potter film.

On Friday, November 23, a special advance screening of *Harry Potter and the Philosopher's Stone* was scheduled. Newly re-elected Australian Premier Peter Beattie and several specially invited guests gathered at Platform 3 (renamed Platform 9¾ for the occasion) at Roma Street Station in Brisbane and awaited the 3:20 arrival of a Queensland Railroad Heritage steam train (disguised as the Hogwarts Express). The train arrived on schedule, picked up the premier and his guests, and departed for Warner Bros. Movie World at 4:00.

Amongst the guests were politicians, TV and radio personalities, senior corporate leaders, and prizewinners from all parts of Australia. Arriving at Movie World the invitees followed a red carpet to the Roxy Cinema on Main Street where at 5:30 the much-anticipated premiere flashed onto the silver screen.

In addition to the premiere showing of *Harry Potter and the Philosopher's Stone*, the Warner Bros. special effects department established a "mystically themed" dining venue and a "sumptuous buffet." A laser light show, punctuated with pyrotechnics, added to the magical atmosphere of that night.

On December 26, 2001, a month after the Australasian general premiere of *Harry Potter and the Philosopher's Stone*, the Potter attraction opened at Movie World.

Potterphiles came in droves, with their first stop usually at the Harry Potter Gift Shop halfway down Main Street staffed by young people dressed as generic characters from the books and film. They would then proceed to the queue at Platform 9¾ on the other side of the park, across from the building hosting Wild West Burgers and Vintage Portraits, and admire the Hogwarts Express re-creation. As they queued near the replica, small groups were admitted into a room constructed with brick walls. Their guide, dressed as a Hogwarts student, used his wand to slide the wall open to reveal Diagon Alley—not unlike the scene in the movie when Hagrid first introduces young Harry to the wonders of the wizarding world.

Visitors could now wander into a fully themed, though indoor, Diagon Alley, with all its captivating sets from the film and enhanced with actual movie props. The street was much narrower than the movie set, but held the same wonder and excitement. Though the stores were façades and could not be entered, visitors could peer into the windows of Ollivander's Wand Shop ("Makers of fine wands since 382 BC"), gaze upon the latest racing brooms at Quidditch Supplies, and marvel at Gringott's Bank and its famous pillars. Farther on they could browse the books at Flourish and Blotts, learn how to send an owl using an actual bird from Eeylops Owl Emporium, and visit the Gryffindor Common Room (though this was not actually located in Diagon Alley in the books or film). There was also a retail store where Harry Potter keepsakes were available for purchase. Witches and wizards of all shapes and sizes added to the magic with their special appearances.

Throughout the Christmas holiday period every child visiting Movie World received a free Harry Potter collector movie poster, with the chance to collect two more inside the park.

In mid-2002, with the premiere of *Harry Potter and the Chamber of Secrets,* the attraction was modified. Changes were made, including the addition of a blue Ford Anglia, the much-battered car owned by Arthur Weasley that had been pilfered by his son Ron and Harry Potter when they found themselves without a way to get to Hogwarts for the opening term.

Harry Potter and the Chamber of Secrets created box office history in Australia, grossing $2.3 million in one day. The film was the fourth biggest opening film of all time in Australian box office history.

Despite the success of the books and films, the Harry Potter Movie Magic Experience was not enough of a draw and it closed early in 2003 to be replaced in September by the Official Matrix Exhibit. Like the Harry Potter experience, the new attraction featured props and costumes from the movies and allowed guests to immerse themselves in the world of the Matrix franchise. In September 2007, it too was replaced with the introduction of a set of bumper cars and an arcade attraction—a sad substitution for the exciting attractions it succeeded.

CHAPTER THREE

HARRY POTTER: THE EXHIBITION

It had become apparent to Warner Bros., with the success of the Harry Potter component of Warner Bros. Movie Magic in Australia, that they were sitting on a gold mine. With more than $4.5 billion in worldwide box office gross sales to date, they realized something had to be done to respond to fandom's desire for more Harry Potter and to sustain fan interest between films. The producers of the movies at the time had carefully preserved all the costumes, sets, and props used in the first films, as they were certain they would need them again in subsequent Harry Potter films. As negotiations were still ongoing for the building of a theme park, it could be several years before the artifacts could be properly displayed to the public in that kind of venue, if they were at all. A different solution was needed.

Global Experience Specialists (GES) was already working with Warner Bros. on special projects and promoting films. Eddie Newquist, chief creative officer for GES, later stated that being in the exhibition business he felt that "there's definitely something here." He continued: "Warner Bros. had thought about it, but couldn't really bring it to the front of their minds, and nor could the filmmakers because they were very busy. So, the idea was out there for a number of years, but it didn't really quite click, I think, until Warner Bros. and the filmmakers could see some sort of end in sight and say, 'Well, what do we do with all these amazing things, and how do we share this in a special way?' We were kind of in the right place at the right time and the filmmakers were in the right place, and it all came together from there."

The exhibitors felt privileged to have Warner Bros. full support in that they could have almost anything they wanted. Whenever they asked, "Can we have that?" the reply was usually ,"Yes, of course."

GES had to be mindful that the films were still in production. They met with executives David Heyman, David Barron, and Stuart Craig, who helped with the designs and contributed great ideas. Newquist recalled: "But then we met with the different heads of the departments, from costumes to props and other things and we'd say, 'Well, maybe we should have that,' and they were like, 'No. We can't tell you why, but you can't have that.' We said, 'Oh, okay. Wink, we get it.'"

As ideas for the exhibition began to expand, they brought everything out to the Great Hall set, which was the largest available space at Leavesden, and laid them out. Using white gloves as they would for real artifacts ("because we wanted these to last for the next hundred years"), everything was tagged and inventoried.

A challenge they faced was with the interactive exhibits, in particular how to involve the quaffle balls used in Quidditch. Newquist explained: "It took a number of months of trial and error to come up with quaffles that felt like real quaffles, that would move like real quaffles."

He knew that millions of people would be tossing and handling the balls as the exhibition toured. The original molds that were used for the film quaffles were used for the exhibition balls, as were the molds for the mandrakes in the Herbology display.

Once all the props that would be used in the exhibition had been selected, GES had to get them to the first venue in Chicago. Some of the items were shipped in large containers, others went by air. Once in the United States they were loaded into 16 semi trucks. Newquist said: "They're all air-ride vehicles; we pay a lot of attention to making sure the temperature is appropriate. We have to watch the paper very carefully."

During the exhibition some of the items wore out or faded, so GES would contact Warner Bros. and exchange them for new ones. As the films were released over the length of the tour, new items could be added.

In late April 2008 Warner Bros. Consumer Products, in partnership with GES and Becker Group, announced it would bring to worldwide audiences Harry Potter: The Exhibition, a state-of-the-art exhibition highlighting artifacts from the Warner Bros. films based on J.K. Rowling's series of books.

David Heyman, producer of the Harry Potter films, said: "Since 2000, when we began production on the adaptation of the first of Jo Rowling's remarkable books, we have had the great privilege of working with some of the most talented artists and craftsman in the world. We are delighted that fans will finally have the opportunity to see, in person, some of their favorite props and costumes. We are looking forward to audiences enjoying the care, creativity and attention to detail involved in their making, just as we do each and every day on set."

Initially, Harry Potter: The Exhibition was to be housed in a 10,000-square-foot space and was to be shown in ten cities around the world over a span of five years.

According to the press release, Harry Potter: The Exhibition would include "elaborate displays of authentic costumes, props and artifacts from popular environments featured in the films such as those from Hogwarts School of Witchcraft and Wizardry, including the Gryffindor Common Room and Hagrid's hut."

As more films were produced and released, the exhibit would be updated to include artifacts from the final Harry Potter films. At the time of the announcement for Harry Potter: The Exhibition, *Harry Potter and the Half-Blood Prince* was still in production and slated for release on November 21, 2008.

The exhibition would be displayed in "major cultural and entertainment venues, museums and institutions, and...supported by a multimedia promotional effort."

Glenn Tilley, president and chief executive officer of Becker Group, stated: "Creating this magical tour around such a legendary property is a true milestone for Becker Group, both as a company and a source of creative entertainment-based attractions."

Brad Globe, president Warner Bros. Consumer Products, added: "We're thrilled to partner with Becker Group to produce this multi-dimensional exhibition dedicated to the iconic

Harry Potter film series. Fans around the world will finally be able to see the incredible craftsmanship and detail that went into creating their favorite props and costumes."

Harry Potter: The Exhibition was not the first time these two partners had collaborated.

Warner Bros. and Becker Group had previously worked together on the successful Happy Feet Snow Globe Experience, the Fred Claus Snow Globe Experience and the classic holiday film *The Polar Express*.

The Becker Group is a subsidiary of Viad Corp and described itself as an "experiential marketing company with over fifty years of experience creating immersive, entertaining attractions and brand-based experiences for a wide variety of clients" including "top consumer brands, movie studios, retail centers, television networks, theme parks, museums and casinos around the globe."

By the time Harry Potter: The Exhibition opened, the floor space had expanded to 15,000 square feet and the number of venues to fifteen, though that information was not necessarily shared with the public at the time. The world premiere was in Chicago, Illinois, in April 2009, and the exhibition was scheduled to continue an extensive tour that would include Boston, Toronto, Seattle, New York, Sydney, Singapore, Tokyo, Edmonton, Sweden, Cologne, Paris, Shanghai, Brussels, and Utrecht. After its final scheduled stop, the tour would continue to additional unannounced international cultural and entertainment venues, museums, and institutions.

Warner Bros. let it be known that the first artifact in Harry Potter: The Exhibition to arrive in Chicago's Museum of Science and Industry on South Lake Shore Drive was the flying Ford Anglia from *Harry Potter and the Chamber of Secrets*. It was the first of more than 200 costumes, artifacts, and props that would arrive at the museum for the world premiere of Harry Potter: The Exhibition. Over 3,000 man-hours were put into the setup and transfer of all original artifacts from the Harry Potter films, straight from the studios at Leavesden where much of the principal photography for the Harry Potter films was shot.

Press releases explained that nearly 6,000 pounds of cables, rigging, lighting, speakers, and assorted special effects were what brought the exhibition to life. Several years of collaboration between film makers and exhibitors was required.

Timed-entry tickets were essential, and the last entry would be from 30 minutes to one hour before the closing of the exhibition, depending on the venue. An exclusive audio tour was also available, providing behind-the-scenes insight into the making of the Harry Potter films, with commentary from the producers, prop designers, costume designers, and creature designers.

Producers David Heyman and David Barron, production designer Stuart Craig, and director David Yates provided their stories on certain props for the audio tour of the exhibit. Other department heads, such as costume designer Jany Tenim, talk about some of their favorite pieces as well.

James and Oliver Phelps, who portrayed the Weasley twins George and Frank, had been asked to go to Chicago some time before the exhibition started to make the announcement. They stayed in touch with GES and periodically they would be asked, "We've got an opening. Would you like to come to it?" As they did more and more of them, they became the most knowledgeable of the cast about what was in the exhibition and so were frequently asked to do the openings. Oliver remarked: "We love coming to different places around the world to talk about it. It never gets old as well, seeing the fans' reaction when they see it for the first time, how excited they are."

The first exhibition in Chicago ran from April 30 to September 27, 2009, at the Museum of Science and Industry. As many of the exhibitions remained the same throughout the tour, we will begin with an extensive look at Harry Potter: The Exhibition as it was first presented.

A preview of the exhibition and a roundtable discussion with its creators was afforded special guests from the more prominent Potter fan websites including The Leaky Cauldron, Dan Radcliffe, MuggleNet, and HPANA (Harry Potter Automatic News Aggregator) one day before the official opening.

A distinct section of the museum had been built to the express needs and desires of the creators of the exhibition. A special set of doors opened into the exhibition and 50 guests at a time were welcomed into the first area, the Sorting Hat. A few volunteers were selected and after sitting on a stool with the Sorting Hat held over their heads by an appropriately dressed witch were sorted into the various houses.

The next area contained eight rectangular framed video screens hung vertically like portraits. Here, to the accompaniment of the strains of "Hedwig's Theme," a brief series of scenes from the already released Harry Potter films was shown to prepare guests for what lay ahead. The guide then took them into a small room where moving, talking portraits lined the walls. After that there was a shrill train whistle as the wall to the left slowly lifted and guests stepped through the true entrance to the exhibition to stand on Platform 9¾ alongside the smoke puffing Hogwarts Express.

The next room was a replica of the Gryffindor Common Room, with many props, including the beds and school robes used by Harry and Ron in the films on display. Other props included their Muggle clothes, their wands, and Harry's glasses. Ron's side of the wall was lined with Chudley Cannon posters while Harry's trunk lay open at the foot of his bed, displaying items such as the discarded box of love potion-spiked chocolates from Romilda Vane, and the Marauders' Map.

Hereafter the exhibition was arranged in corridors, with walls draped in black curtains to make every scene separate. Props abounded: a list of the members of Dumbledore's army, a book on Do-It-Yourself Broomcare, the howler (both open and closed) that Ron's mother sent him after he used the Ford Anglia without permission, Harry's acceptance letter to Hogwarts, the golden egg that Harry retrieved from the dragon pit during the Triwizard Tournament, and a bottle of Pumpkin Juice.

From the (as then) unreleased *Harry Potter and the Half-Blood Prince*, there was Professor Slughorn's costume along with an appropriate display of potions including a box labelled and containing bezoars and two editions of Liberatius Borage's *Advanced Potion Making*. Nearby was the Divination display complete with a teacup containing tea leaves in the shape of the Grim.

Straight from *Harry Potter and the Chamber of Secrets* was the Gilderoy Lockhart display with numerous poses of the eccentric Defence Against the Dark Arts teacher used for signed autographs and book covers. The portrait of Lockhart painting a portrait of himself that appeared in the DADA (Defene Against the Dark Arts) classroom in the film served as a backdrop. The DADA Second-Year Essential Knowledge Test reposed in a glass case with the questions based on Lockhart himself seen only in the deleted scenes.

Professor Dolores Umbridge's office from *Harry Potter and the Order of the Phoenix* was resplendent with a wall filled with cat plates, her robes, and wand. The other DADA professors were also allotted their own display corners, with Remus Lupin's space dominated by a Boggart rattling about in an old wardrobe.

One of the most popular features of Harry Potter: The Exhibition was the hands-on display area. There was a table from Professor Pomona Sprout's Herbology class complete with mandrakes that screeched as the guest pulled them part way out of their pots. An adult mandrake's scream could cause death, but these infant versions were merely annoying, and though the students in *Harry Potter and the Chamber of Secrets* were provided with earmuffs, they were not required in the exhibition. The molds for the mandrakes were based on the actual plant, but the designers had to take care not to make the seedlings too cute becauser they were destined to be harvested to provide a cure for the petrification inflicted on some of the students. More than fifty animatronic mandrakes were created for the film, from which a handful were designed to be lifted from their pots; a few of these were used in the exhibition.

Quidditch was represented as guests passed through a tent entrance to see the uniforms worn by Bulgaria and Ireland at the World Cup Tournament from *Harry Potter and the Goblet of Fire*. The uniforms of Ron and Harry from *Harry Potter and the Half-Blood Prince* were also there as well as a quaffle, bludger, and intricate Golden Snitch. A second hands-on display allowed visitors to demonstrate their skill at tossing the red, leathery quaffle through a Quidditch goal hoop. A successful toss was rewarded by a ring of success from the Hogwarts Quidditch pitch bell.

Hagrid's Hut contained a massive costume designed for the Keeper of Keys and Grounds at Hogwarts. The dimensions of the hut, including the size and much of the interior, were identical to that of the "real" hut in the films. A sign invited visitors to sit in his massive chair from where they could see the fireplace and on a table beside it a slightly cracked, wiggling egg. One could also see Hagrid's pink umbrella, a copy of the *Monster Book of Monsters*, and assorted crates and knick-knacks cluttering the area.

There was also a replica Buckbeak, an eagle-headed equine, just outside Hagrid's Hut. The front half of the Hippogriff was covered in died feathers, all applied by hand and so realistic that most guests, familiar with the proper etiquette taught by Hagrid, gave the beast a bow before approaching. Three life-sized Hippogriffs had been created for *Harry Potter and the Prisoner of Azkaban*. One was for foreground shots, one for background shots, and the third to sit in the pumpkin patch outside Hagrid's Hut. A fourth Buckbeak was created digitally for whenever a shot of the creature walking or in flight was required.

The rooms darkened as visitors moved on and into the Forbidden Forest. A scented fog machine gave the area a damp and earthy smell and the sound and lighting gave the impression of entering a forest. A young Thestral, Centaurs, a Hungarian Horntail, and some of Aragog's offspring guarded displays of Tom Riddle's school uniform and a diary impaled with a basilisk fang. Props from various films became intermixed with the Triwizard Cup and two chess pieces from the full-sized game the trio played to advance toward the Philosopher's (Sorcerer's) Stone. Wanted posters for Bellatrix LeStrange and Amycus and Alecto Carrow hung suspended near a Dementor. The Angel of Death statue from the graveyard scene in *Harry Potter and the Goblet of Fire* was represented under a Dark Mark high in the sky.

Relieved to be out of the darkness, visitors now entered the Great Hall decorated with Umbridge's imposing educational decrees and some of Headmaster Albus Dumbledore's costumes. This final area of the exhibition featured a long table laden with replica foods, desserts, and candies from Honeydukes. In addition, there was a case of jokes and games from Zonko's and Weasley's. There was also a naked Dobby which was used as a study model in *Harry Potter and the Chamber of Secrets* to make it possible for graphic artists to properly render him. He was clothed for later exhibitions. One corner was dedicated to the Yule Ball where Ron's ancient and flowery dress robes and Hermione's gown are displayed along with the other champions' costumes and the ice sculpture centerpiece.

Some twenty-five costumes were represented in the exhibition including that of the Bloody Baron, a must-see as it barely makes an appearance in the films. The costumes worn by Harry, Ron, and Hermione in the early films were there, surprisingly small until one remembers they were worn by pre-teens.

At the end of the exhibition was the obligatory gift shop where eager fans could purchase books, movies, buttons, busts, action figures, and many of the other multitudinous merchandise items, some of which were exclusive to the exhibition.

The exhibition at the Museum of Science and Industry in Chicago proved so popular that the hours were extended in its final weeks in response to sold-out weekends. On one day in mid-June, almost 20,000 people checked out the displays. On September 18, hours were extended until midnight on Friday and Saturday nights. David Mosena, president and CEO of the museum, stated: "Hundreds of thousands of Harry Potter fans have been captivated by this exhibition, and by extending our weekend hours, we hope many more will have the opportunity to do so before it leaves Chicago."

Less than a month later, Harry Potter: The Exhibition moved to the East Coast and opened at the Museum of Science in Boston, Massachusetts. Again, noted Potterphiles were invited to an early preview and a round-table chat with actor Matthew Lewis who portrayed Neville Longbottom in the films.

Opening on October 25, 2009, the exhibition proved to be as popular in Boston as it was in Chicago, as confirmed by the 30,000 people who made a special trip, despite the cold and snow, to check it out. It was so popular that museum staff sometimes had to bend the rules to accommodate everyone. One staffer noted that we were "only supposed to let 50 people into the exhibit at a time and then keep those groups spaced 5 minutes apart, but things got so busy and so crazy during the Christmas vacation week that we sometimes had to bump up that number from 50 to 60 people. Which made things really hot and crowded inside of the exhibit area. But that at least allowed us to get the line outside back under control."

As the end of the exhibition approached, hours were extended and another week added to the schedule, moving the end date to February 28, 2010.

The next stop was at the Ontario Science Centre in Toronto, Canada, from April 9 to September 6, 2010. Once again, the Weasley twins, Fred and George, portrayed by James and Oliver Phelps, made an appearance and opened the exhibition.

Eddie Newquist and Robin Stapley, creators of the exhibition, revealed "that it took about 16 semi-trucks to import everything across the Canada-United States border." Even though they had been gathering props and items for the exhibition for over two years, the only major challenge they had encountered, so far, was the large amount of material that there was to shift from place to place.

The Ontario Science Centre had been chosen for the first Canadian exhibition because "the foundation of science comes from inspiration; and just as Harry Potter has a long history of ideas, science also has a long history of ideas." Though no more hands-on exhibits were planned due to the sensitive nature of many of the artifacts, it was the intention of the creators of the exhibition to add props from *Harry Potter and the Deathly Hallows* as they became available.

Again, the popularity of the exhibition led to its run being extended for an additional two weeks before being transported west and back across the border to Seattle, Washington. The Pacific Science Center was slated to host the exhibition from October 23, 2010, to January 30, but as with previous exhibitions, the closing date was extended, this time to February 13, 2011.

Though Harry Potter: The Exhibition had originally been scheduled for only four North American shows, a fifth was added, in New York City's Discovery Times Square, to run from April 5 to September 5, 2011. Warner Bros. announced that the exhibition would be holding a special Sneak Peek Weekend (April 1-3) before the official opening. The press release stated: "The previously unscheduled stop in New York City will serve as the tour's final North American destination before going international."

On the day before the grand opening, a red-carpet event was held for the press and a number of cast members in attendance, including David Barron (producer), Robbie Coltrane (Hagrid), Warwick Davis (Griphook/Flitwick), Michael Gambon (Dumbledore), Domhnall Gleeson (Bill Weasley), David Heyman (producer). Evanna Lynch (Luna Lovegood), Helen McCrory (Narcissa Malfoy), James Phelps (Fred Weasley), Oliver Phelps (George Weasley), Clémence Poésy (Fleur Delacour), Freddie Stroma (Cormac McLaggen), Natalia Tena (Nymphadora Tonks), David Thewlis (Remus Lupin), Mark Williams (Arthur Weasley), and Bonnie Wright (Ginny Weasley).

Many suspected that the next stop for the exhibition would be somewhere in Europe, but instead it was the Powerhouse Museum in Sydney, Australia. James and Oliver Phelps were again at the opening event for the show that ran from November 19, 2011 to April 9, 2012.

Logistically, the move to Australia had been the most daunting to date. The exhibition had to first travel overland from New York to Los Angeles where it was loaded onto 23 shipping containers which took 40 days to get from Los Angeles to Sydney.

Harry Potter and the Deathly Hallows: Part 2 had been released in July 2011, and though the exhibition had not changed its overall layout or content, it now had access to props from the last two films. All the horcruxes, for example, were now in the exhibit, including the snake, Nagini, though not Harry (Oliver Phelps suggested they could lock Dan Radcliffe in a cabinet). The Deathly Hallows are also all together for the first time. Hermione's red dress that she wore at Bill and Fleur's wedding was on display, as were the clothes worn by Harry, Ron, Luna, and Xenophilius. Neville Longbottom's sweater and the Sword of Gryffindor were placed, appropriately, side by side. Death Eater costumes and their accompanying wands were also in evidence.

Before the exhibition departed from Australia, the 2012 New South Wales Tourism Awards were announced and the exhibition won the Sun Herald Reader's Choice Award.

From Sydney, the exhibition put to sea again, for the port city of Singapore where it was scheduled to run from June 2 to September 30, 2012, at the ArtScience Museum at Marina Bat Sands. The Phelps twins were there for opening day. The venue was almost identical to the earlier exhibitions, except that the entrance was through a dimly lit passage and a curtain of mist leading to the Sorting Hat room where two lovely witches waited.

A month later Harry Potter: The Exhibition was back in New York City, returning to Discovery Times Square for a stay from November 2, 2012, to April 7, 2013. James and Oliver Phelps were on hand, signing autographs outside the main entrance, with the line to meet them snaking down the street for most of the day despite the freezing weather.

The ninth stop of the tour was Roppongi Hills in Tokyo, Japan, at the Mori Arts Center Gallery. Every relocation had its challenges and every facility was different. Frank Torres, one of the exhibition creators, told an interviewer: "Obviously going from one country to the other, you have rules and regulations you have to follow, transportation, sizes of trucks and how you can get them into a city, how you get into a building. For example, in Tokyo we were in the 52nd floor of a building, so...one piece at a time. ... There's a lot of planning that goes into each one of these venues. It's usually about a six-month process from once we identify where we're going, then I go forward and I'll visit those locations and do a preliminary How are we going to get in here? What will we need? What kind of trucks? and then you just move on from there."

The exhibition ran from June 22 to September 29, 2013. Few changes were made, though all the exhibitions were slightly different in layout due to the differences in configuration of the space available. The Sorting Hat room in Tokyo, for example, was a big black room with posters from all the movies and a stained-glass window behind the sorting hat giving the appearance of a small version of the Great Hall. Some of the props would be arranged differently and some of the potions, when shipped internationally, raised questions from Customs and had to be checked. Due to popular demand from fans, the exhibition in Tokyo was extended another two weeks.

The tenth stop, and originally the last of the five-year tour, was at the Edmonton Telus World of Science Centre in Edmonton, Alberta, Canada, from November 23, 2013, to April 6, 2014. The Phelps twins, of course, were there. George Smith, president and CEO of Telus World of Science, remarked: "Harry Potter has enthralled fans worldwide as it stimulates their creativity and imaginations. Bringing Harry Potter: The Exhibition to Edmonton is exciting. Providing world-class entertainment to the people of Edmonton and Alberta is essential as our community continues to grow and attract people from around the globe."

Due to restrictions on space, some of the larger props were placed in different locations. One chess piece was in the Telus World of Science lobby, the knight piece that Ron rode was located in the Edmonton International Airport, just past security, and the Ford Anglia was at Kingsway Mall where tickets for the exhibition could be purchased.

Though the exhibition was originally scheduled to end on March 9, the run was extended by almost a month to April 6 to allow more visitors to experience it before a scheduled European tour. During that additional month, visitors were given the opportunity to win one of the replica quaffles or a souvenir poster signed by James and Oliver Phelps.

By the time Harry Potter: The Exhibition departed Edmonton, more than three million people from around the globe had experienced the magic of Harry Potter through authentic film props, sets, costumes, and creatures.

The eleventh venue, and the start of the European part of the exhibition tour, began in Norrköping, Sweden, at the multi-purpose stadium of Nya Parken, on May 19 until September 17, 2014. Stefan Papangelis, CEO of Experience Norrköping with whom GES was partnering, stated: "We are honored to be the first city in Europe to host this stunning exhibition. We couldn't be more excited to welcome all Harry Potter fans to Norrköping."

The Odysseum, a high-tech and interactive science and technology museum aimed at children, was the site of the twelfth Harry Potter: The Exhibition in Cologne, Germany, from October 3, 2014, to March 1, 2015. MinaLima, the graphic design artists behind the Harry Potter films, released a limited-edition fine art print to coincide with the launch. The collectors' print was available for purchase at the retail shop and was the first print produced by MinaLima exclusively for the touring exhibition.

The next venue was at La Cité Du Cinéma, Film Set 8 & 9, in Saint-Denis, Paris, France, from April 4 to September 6, 2015. The entrance to the venue had a different atmosphere as a beautiful rendition of Hogwarts Castle took up a large portion of a wall, made even more interesting by the lights illuminating some of the windows. Movie posters from the films lined the entranceway and the strains of John Williams' Harry Potter score enhanced the magical feeling of the place.

The tour ended with in China. The 9th floor of the China Super Brand Mall in Lujiazui, Shanghai, was hosted the exhibition from December 5, 2015, to February 28, 2016. The Van Egmond Group partnered with GES to present the exhibition in Shanghai.

The exhibition was back in Europe again within a few months of the Shanghai closing. This time the venue was Belgium Brussels Expo in Brussels, from June 30 to November 6, 2016. The Phelps twins were present for the opening and new additions were advertised. The Ford Anglia, which had been in Edmonton but not at the exhibition, was again part of the show, as was the Wizard Chess set, first introduced in Shanghai. The interior was decorated for Christmas with trees, wreaths, and artificial snow.

A brand-new vignette of props and costumes from Warner Bros. latest film, *Fantastic Beasts and Where to Find Them*, attracted a great deal of attention. Amongst the moving paintings introduced in the first exhibition was a new one of Newt Scamander as well as a wanted poster featuring Newt and his Muggle friend, Jacob Kowalski. A copy of *Transfiguration Today*, an Occamy egg, and a pair of wands were displayed on a table. Nearby was a poster for the film and the costume of Newt Scamander with the dresses of Tina and Queenie Goldstein on ether side of it.

The exhibition closed as scheduled on November 6 and reopened at Palais 2, also in Brussels, on the following

Saturday, November 17, 2016, and ran until January 8, 2017. The exhibition had welcomed more than 275,000 guests since it opened in Brussels on June 30 and topped four million worldwide.

James Phelps, who played Fred Weasley, attended the second opening along with the winner of a Facebook contest that gave fans a chance to win an opportunity to join him at the official opening.

The sixteenth showing of Harry Potter: The Exhibition was held at CineMec in Utrecht, Netherlands, from February 11, 2017 until June 30, 2017.

Outside the venue, large posters of Daniel Radcliffe, Emma Watson, and Rupert Grint were hung. The area was a bit out of the way, but it was custom made for the exhibition. Frank Torres said: "Here it was a custom-made venue for us, for the first time, so it was absolutely perfect. The ceiling heights are just right, the walls are designed so you feel really immersed, it's very cozy, and the sound is great because we have so much drapery keeping the sound in each area."

A battered flying Ford Anglia was the first prop visitors saw as they entered the CineMac building. Farther on they could have a photo taken against a variety of Harry Potter-themed backgrounds. Next came the familiar Sorting Hat room and Platform 9¾ with the rest of the exhibition as shown previously. At one time it had been suggested that the entire chess set from *Harry Potter and the Philosopher's Stone* scene be used, but realistically, as James Phelps noted: "You can see just how tall they actually are, but they'd probably have to use the Amsterdam Arena to hold it all in because it's so big."

The tour premiered in Chicago in 2009, and now the global tour has been extended again to run until spring 2020. Future venues have yet to be announced. Freddie Newquist hinted at something in the future when he talked about *Fantastic Beasts and Where to Find Them* costumes in Brussels, saying: "We have dreams and ideas, but we can't say anything official right now."

CHAPTER FOUR
BUILDING A WIZARDING WORLD

The origins of the Wizarding World theme park are shrouded in mystery, conjecture, rumors, wishful thinking, and a few known facts. To begin, it should be noted that while Warner Bros. had the film and merchandising rights to Harry Potter, they did not have any major theme parks. The rival studios of Universal and Disney, however, each had extensive and successful theme parks and both were interested in obtaining the park rights for Harry Potter. This narrowed the playing field considerably, as only those two, of all the theme parks in the United States, had deep enough pockets to both obtain the rights and then to build the new park. It was now up to Walt Disney Imagineering and Universal Creative to draw up their proposals and submit them to J.K. Rowling and others involved in the negotiations.

There was a story floating around the internet in 2003 regarding Disney and Harry Potter. Apparently, Bob Gault, president of Universal Orlando, was in the habit of holding a "Lunch with Bob" question-and-answer period for his executives to ask questions about various ongoing or future projects. It was a sort of brainstorming session that often resulted in promising ideas coming forward and Gault assigning people to follow up on them.

According to an online correspondent known as H.C., at the July 3 session Gault was asked one question in particular that is of interest here: "Has Universal pursued Lord of the Rings or Harry Potter?"

"Disney has Harry Potter wrapped up. We will check into Lord of the Rings," Gault is said to have replied.

The source of this report wondered if Gault had misspoken by stating that "Disney has Harry Potter wrapped up" and multitudes of Harry Potter, Universal, and Disney fans wanted to know for sure. Blogger Jim Hill felt duty bound to get to the bottom of the rumour and began making phone calls to everyone and anyone who might know the answer.

One thing he learned was that "a few years back, Universal was positively desperate to acquire the theme park rights to the Harry Potter characters. So much so that Universal Creative [the folks who actually design all of the rides, shows and attractions for the Universal theme parks] put together a proposal for a Harry Potter-themed stunt show."

The hope was that the idea would be presented to Rowling and she would be so enthralled with the project that she would award the rights to a Harry Potter theme park to Universal. The proposal was to be "a special effects filled extravaganza, loosely modeled after that theme park's Wild, Wild, Wild West stunt show." The finale would be a duel between Harry, Ron, Hermione, and Lord Voldemort. The scene was not based on anything from any of the books or films that had been done to date, but was to be "a stand-alone show" based on the style and flavor of the books rather than an actual event from the story. Lots of wand waving, spell casting, sparkling fireworks, explosions, and blazing fires would lead up to the climatic destruction of the Dark Lord.

As it happened, Universal Creative never had an opportunity to present their proposal, for when they approached Rowlings' representatives they were told, "We've already awarded the theme park rights to someone else."

Naturally, the assumption was that "someone else" must be Disney. Hill reported, however, that despite numerous conversations with Walt Disney Imagineering insiders, no one would admit to a Disney and Harry Potter connection. He wrote: "The closest I ever got to confirmation was a couple of knowing smiles from veteran Imagineers as well as a 'Sorry, but that would be telling' from someone in the studio's legal department.

Such secrecy is certainly not unknown amongst studio corporate giants for a variety of reasons. Hill cites the secret talks with George Lucas about the Star Tours and Indiana Jones attractions at Disneyland as examples not only of secrecy but the use of non-Disney characters in the theme parks. Nothing else was found and the story slowly disappeared.

Hill later reported, in October 2006, that Disney was negotiating with Rowling about a theme park project: "After months of negotiations, Rowling finally signed a letter of intent which then awarded The Walt Disney Company the right to begin preliminary development of a theme park-related project featuring the Harry Potter characters."

Though this statement was refuted by a representative for Rowling, Hill stuck by his original statement, saying that he could not go into too much detail as that would reveal his source.

Keeping in mind that a letter of intent is merely an acknowledgement between companies that they are willing and able to do business and is not a legal or binding document, it is quite possible that such a document may have existed.

Another theme park blogger, Robert Niles, added to the mystique with an interview he had with Disney Imagineer Tony Baxter in September 2015. Niles asked Baxter about future theme park developments. Baxter replied: "Well, the biggest misstep—well, we've got to be careful how we say this one—I won't say a word, but it looks a lot like this." He then stood and picked up a large booklet from his desk titled *Walt Disney Imagineering: Harry Potter Plans*.

Rumour had it that J. K. Rowling was being "rather demanding" in her negotiations with Disney and was "making unrealistic demands" to the point that "Phase One of Disney's Harry Potter park would just make this project fiscally irresponsible as well as an operational nightmare." It has also been reported that Rowling had very definite plans for the project. Apparently, she wanted "guests to enter through Diagon Alley, then board the Hogwarts Express for a trip to Harry's school." This sounds great, on paper, but could become a guest flow nightmare.

While it is possible that Disney and Rowling signed a letter of intent, it is also known that Disney acquired the rights to broadcast the Harry Potter movies. A small controversy erupted when ABC wanted to spilt the televising of the films over two nights "since most kids can't stay up until 11 p.m. and they can pack more internal commercials into the movie. But they're balking at pre-empting regular programming on a Sunday during May sweeps." Perhaps it was this publicity that led to people mistakenly thinking the letter of intent referred to a theme park when it fact it was all about televising the movies.

How much truth there is in those statements is unimportant as the fact is that Disney CEO Bob Iger made obtaining Pixar his focus instead of Harry Potter, and Rowling began talking to the people at Universal. As it turned out, the deal was anything but "fiscally irresponsible" for Universal nor would it have been for Disney, but they soon had their Imagineers fully engaged with the latest attraction for Disney's California Adventure, Cars Land.

In January 2007, a rumor from a "highly credible source" surfaced online that the Lost Continent area of Islands of Adventure in Universal Orlando would be rethemed to "one of the most popular children's franchises." Other sources suggested that it was the Harry Potter movies that were being developed under the code name "Project Strong Arm," a reference to the KUKA robotic system that would be used for the major attraction. Other media sources soon began to speculate about this new park.

Meanwhile, executives from both Warner Bros. and Universal had flown to Edinburgh to meet with Rowling in the Caledonian Hotel. It was very much a case of Hollywood going to her rather than her going to Hollywood. They had gone to Scotland to discuss the theme park in Orlando and were seeking Rowlings' approval. "The plans I've seen look incredibly exciting, and I don't think fans of the books or films will be disappointed," she said.

Then it was Rowlings' turn to inspect the proposed site for the Wizarding World. She is said to have been very impressed by the extensive detail found in the Enchanted Oak Tavern in the Lost Continent, the kind of detail needed to bring her characters to life. But it was reportedly Seuss Landing that clinched the deal. Rowling had heard about the great lengths that Universal had gone to keep Dr. Seuss' widow,

Audrey Dimond, happy, when Seuss Landing was being built. Whatever she had asked for, she got, whatever condition she set, they met, whatever color she wanted, they painted, whatever restaurant she asked for, they built, wherever she wanted it. Rowling liked the sound of that and decided these were the people who could build her Wizarding World.

Speculation about who owned the Harry Potter theme park rights was finally put to rest in a press release from Universal on May 31, 2007. The plan was not for a single attraction but a new land at Universal Studios Orlando's Islands of Adventure to be called the Wizarding World of Harry Potter. The press release stated: "The fully immersive, themed land will enable guests to visit some of the most iconic locations found in the books and the films, including the village of Hogsmeade, the mysterious Forbidden Forest, and even Hogwarts castle itself."

Beyond that the press release provided few specific details. No opening date, except for 2010, was mentioned, and the attractions were vaguely described as "immersive rides and interactive attractions, as well as experiential shops and restaurants that will enable guests to sample fare from the wizarding world's best-known establishments. Also debuting will be a state-of-the-art attraction that will bring the magic, characters, and stories of Harry Potter to life in an exciting way that guests have never before experienced."

Chairman and CEO of Universal Parks and Resorts Tom Williams promised: "We are going to devote more time, more money, more expertise, and more executive talent from throughout our entire organization and creative team, as well as from Warner Bros., our partners, to ensure that this entire environment is second-to-none." The conceptual renderings that accompanied the press release depicted Hogwarts School of Witchcraft and Wizardry and a snow-covered Hogsmeade which seemed to confirm that guests were in for something spectacular.

The area chosen for the Wizarding World was in Universal's Islands of Adventure between Jurassic Park and the Lost Continent, and as construction grew, part of the Lost Continent area was taken over as well. Steel and concrete would slowly be shaped into Hogwarts Castle as it rose on a rocky prominence in the first major expansion of the Islands of Adventure since the park opened in 1999.

The land had been largely vacant since Islands of Adventure opened except for the Flying Unicorn attraction. At one time plans were drawn up for an attraction to be called Jurassic Park Helicopters. This would tie in nicely with Jurassic Park next door and concept drawing showed an aerial simulator flying over assorted species of dinosaurs. The concept did not progress beyond the drawing board.

Another idea put forth was for a Van Helsing attraction, based on the 2004 Universal film of the same name. The attraction would involve the monster hunter as well as a reinvented Count Dracula who is using Dr. Victor Frankenstein's research and a werewolf for his own sinister purposes. Designed as a dark ride inside a huge show building, it would likely have spread over the entire undeveloped area. The attraction concept was to use KUKA's Robocoaster technology, the same tech that would eventually be used for Harry Potter and the Forbidden Journey.

Universal had wanted to follow in Disney's footsteps and build a second park in Florida since the 1980s. Their first attempt at a theme park, in Hollywood, had been successful, and they felt they could repeat the idea in Florida, just as Disney had done in 1971 with Walt Disney World. Like Disney, they chose central Florida and bought land that Disney had earlier rejected near the intersection of the Florida Turnpike and Interstate 4. It wasn't until 1986 that construction began, a move that Universal claimed prompted Disney to fast-track their Disney-MGM Studios park to a 1989 opening.

Universal Studios Florida's debut on June 7, 1990, was less than stellar. The opening of Disneyland in July 1955 had been termed "Black Sunday" due to the many mishaps that plagued the day, but Universal's opening was worse. Almost none of the park's rides worked. To compensate visitors, and give the park a second chance, everyone who visited was given a complimentary ticket to return on another day.

Over the years the park evolved. Unlike Universal Studios Hollywood, there was no all-encompassing Tram Tour; instead, they relied on stand-alone attractions. Little in the park continued past the initial few years. Only the E.T. ride and Horror Make-Up show survived in anything close to their original form. The ride portion of the Earthquake attraction ditched the pre-ride demonstrations and became Disaster! Most of the other attractions were replaced over the years with newer, usually high-tech, shows and rides such as Transformers: The Ride 3D and The Simpson's Ride, with Springfield's restaurants and bars themed to the TV show.

Despite all the changes inside Universal Studios Florida, the park itself seemed like a model of stability compared to adjacent areas. The original Hard Rock Cafe, built atop a guitar-shaped platform, became the site of the Curious George water playground. Three new hotels, with another under construction; the massive CityWalk shopping-and-dining complex; and two multi-storey parking garages now surround the park. The original parking lot became the site of Islands of Adventure.

Though the site Universal purchased was smaller than Walt Disney World, it was large enough to expand to include another park. An all-cartoon park had been considered, with characters from Warner Bros. and either Marvel or DC Comics since Universal had few characters of their own. Instead, when their own movie, *Jurassic Park*, became a box office hit in 1993, they decided to go in that direction and Islands of Adventure came into being.

Construction began in 1997 and Islands of Adventure officially opened on May 28, 1999, to rave reviews. Unlike the studio theme parks that stuck mainly to Universal's own characters, Islands of Adventure expanded to include other franchises and license multiple properties from other creators. These were to include Jay Ward's Dudley Do-Right, Marvel Comics' Incredible Hulk and Spiderman, King Features' Popeye, Dr. Seuss' Cat in the Hat, and other characters. The Lost Continent was designed by Disney Imagineers who had worked on the proposed, but later dropped, Beastly Kingdom for Disney's Animal Kingdom. Hybrid dark-ride and 3D technology for high-tech attractions became a huge draw.

By 2001 Universal Creative had moved to Orlando from California and the complex was rebranded Universal Orlando

Resort. They managed to weather the global drop in tourism in the early 2000s and came out of it better than any other theme park except for those owned by Disney. But they still needed one more major licensing deal to propel them to another level.

It came in the form of the boy wizard when Universal won the rights from Warner Bros. and Rowling, thanks in part to collaborators like Audrey Stone Dimond, Dr. Seuss' widow. The deal was announced on May 31, 2007, though the official opening date of June 18, 2010, was not announced until March 25, 2010. The ideal place to build Hogsmeade and Hogwarts presented itself in the 20-acre (81,000 m^2) site known as the Lost Continent, part of which the Wizarding World of Harry Potter would usurp.

As part of the promotion for the new park, a behind-the-scenes documentary about its development was included in the Blu-ray and DVD editions of *Harry Potter and the Half-Blood Prince*.

While construction was progressing, a sign resembling a Ministry of Magic proclamation, as seen in *Harry Potter and the Order of the Phoenix*, was set up outside the area:

> Proclamation.
> Ministry Decree
> No. 01
> Magic at Work
> Your Patience
> is
> Requested
> (Ministry of Magic Logo)

At the end of October 2009, an open casting call was made for actors for Wizarding World. Auditions would be held on November 14 and 15 in the Universal Orlando Human Resources lobby. Universal was looking for "male and female actors who can speak with a British accent. More specifically, Universal is holding calls for male actors with strong improv and interaction skills who are able to portray an age range of mid-thirties to mid-forties. In addition, they're casting male and female actors who are youthful in appearance. Full-time, part-time, and seasonal positions are available. All actors should prepare a one-minute monologue for audition and candidates must be available for callbacks on Monday, Nov. 16, and rehearsals beginning in January."

Some of the attractions from the Lost Continent were to be repurposed for use in the Harry Potter land. Dueling Dragons had originally opened with Islands of Adventure in May 1999 in an area known as Merlin Woods. Made by the Swiss manufacturer Bollinger and Mabillard, it was the first and only fully inverted roller coaster in the world at the time and was themed to two dueling dragons named Fire and Ice. Toward the end of 2009, construction began on retheming the queue and removing most of the skeletons, presumably the remnants pf people devoured by the dragons, laying about. In early 2010 the ride was closed for conversion to a Harry Potter theme. Though reopened in March, it kept its original name until mid-June when the Wizarding World section officially opened and it became Dragon Challenge.

The other attraction to be repurposed was Flying Unicorn, a Vekoma roller coaster aimed more at the younger set. Opened in 2000, in Merlin Woods, it was themed around a wizard who had found a unicorn's horn and used it to create the ride. Flying Unicorn was shut down on July 7, 2008, to permit construction of Wizarding World nearby. Its repurposing to a Harry Potter theme was not confirmed until September 2009 when it was announced that it would be renamed Flight of the Hippogriff. It had a soft opening on June 1 and officially opened with the rest of the Wizarding World two weeks later.

In the meantime construction continued, and even though some pre-existing facilities were refurbished, the amount of incredible detail that fans would expect from the Warner Bros. films contributed to the length of time it took to build the park. Stuart Craig, the production designer on the Harry Potter films, oversaw the operation to ensure that the artistic consistency was the same in the Wizarding World park as that which fans saw in the films. He was so involved in the site that Universal Security, seeing a man climbing the hill behind Flying Unicorn, went to arrest him. Moments before they could do so, they were informed of his identity and told that he was checking out the site to find the best place to put Hagrid's Hut.

Speculation was rife as to what would be included in the new land. One rumor involved a revamping of the Eighth Voyage of Sindbad stunt show in which guests would be riding in the Weasley's Ford Anglia, careening through the trees of the Forbidden Forest and soaring over Hogwarts Castle.

Excited fans could not see what was going on behind the construction walls that had been installed all over the Lost Continent. Sometimes they could get close to the fences and sometimes see over them, but in the early stages there was not much to see, save mounds of earth being moved about. At that stage there was not much to see, as the construction crew was still busy prepping the site by removing underbrush from the previously undeveloped part of the park and trucking in fill to spread around what would become Hogwarts Castle.

Once the site had been prepared, construction could begin on the foundations and footings needed to support the huge structures that were expected to be done in January. A buffer zone was installed to keep the fantasy Wizarding World separate from the dangerous dinosaur world of Jurassic Park. Actual construction was slated to start in early spring and Hogwarts Castle topped off within a year of beginning the work. Construction of the castle was officially underway in February 2008 as thousands of pieces of steel were trucked in, hoisted up, and attached in place.

The construction of Hogsmeade and Hogwarts has been compared to a giant Lego kit. Hundreds of construction workers were required to assemble the separate pieces created by Orlando's Nassal Company (a worldwide leader in the fabrication and installation of immersive themed environments) and put them together in the right order and right place. With the massive castle-under-construction sheathed in scaffolding, some of the workers were on platforms hundreds of feet in the air, guiding the heavy crane- winched pieces into place despite wind, lightning, and other hazards. Every tower, battlement, snow-covered roof, and parapet had to be placed exactly right to carry out the forced perspective illusion of an even larger castle. Not only did the workers have to meet the exacting standards of J.K. Rowling, but also of every Harry Potter fan who would visit the park.

In an interview, the president of Universal Creative, Mark Woodbury, stated that Rowling was "a critical part of the process and remained that way throughout everything we did." There was one thing about which she was adamant and that was her characters. There would be no one portraying Harry Potter or Lord Voldemort or any of the characters from her books or films. Most theme parks would have their stock of employees in character costumes, Disney had Mickey Mouse, Pluto, Goofy, Snow White, and Cinderella, Knott's Berry Farm has characters from Peanuts, Universal had Bart and Homer Simpson, but the Wizarding World would have only team members dressed as witch or wizard characters not seen in the books or films.

Universal tantalized fans by sharing imagery on a webcast related to the project. Concept art of Dueling Dragons, now renamed Dragon Challenge, and Flying Unicorn, to be called Flight of the Hippogriff and positioned next to Hagrid's Hut, was shown. But they remained vague about the premiere attraction, Harry Potter and the Forbidden Journey, and its state-of-the-art technology. Instead, they showed only artists' concepts of the entrance to the ride through Hogwarts Castle and the post-ride gift shop.

It was to become Universal's custom to hold press conferences for select reporters before the opening of the Wizarding World attractions. Actors and members of the creative team were invited to answer questions from the press. In addition, a three-day media event was held just prior to opening day as the finishing touches were being put on the attractions. Special viewings were held for Rowling and some of the cast members from the Harry Potter films, including Daniel Radcliffe (Harry Potter), Emma Watson (Hermione Granger), Rupert Grint (Ron Weasley), James and Oliver Phelps (Fred and George Weasley), Robbie Coltrane (Rubeus Hagrid), and Matthew Lewis (Neville Longbottom), were given a guided tour of Hogsmeade. They visited some of the shops, tasted butterbeer at the Three Broomsticks, watched a performance of the Durmstrang/Beauxbatons dancers, marveled at the pre-ride show in Hogwarts, and rode Harry Potter and the Forbidden Journey.

Finally, opening day, Friday, June 18, 2010, arrived. Huge crowds had started arriving in the middle of the night for what promised to be an unforgettable day. The freeway overpasses leading to the parking garages were backed up even before the garages opened. The lines inside the park stretched from the entrance at CityWalk to Wizarding World for an estimated half a mile, and for those at the end of the line, an eight-hour wait. The streets were jam-packed with Harry Potter fans wanting to be the first into the new land and most of all wanting to see and hear the actors from the films who were supposed to be on hand to open the new attraction.

A Hogwarts Express conductor stepped up onto an empty stage in front of a huge reproduction of the letter like the one Harry had received from Hogwarts and greeted the crowd. "In a few moments the Hogwarts Express will be arriving with some very special guests." He went on to say that there were other special guests "from schools across America" who he introduced by school name. Next he introduced a VIM (Very Important Muggle), Bill Davis, president and COO of Universal Orlando Resort, who gave a short speech about how the "Wizarding World of Harry Potter is truly the most spectacular entertainment area ever created in history."

No sooner had Davis finished speaking than a train whistle sounded and the noises of an approaching locomotive, with whistle and steam, heralded the arrival of the special guests. The letter-shaped canvas curtain fell to reveal the entrance to the Wizarding World at Hogsmeade.

One by one members of the Harry Potter films cast came out of Hogsmeade and gathered on the stage: Warwick Davis (Flitwick/Griphook), Bonnie Wright (Ginny Weasley), James and Oliver Phelps (Fred and George Weasley), Matthew Lewis (Neville Longbottom), Tom Felton (Draco Malfoy), Michael Gambon (Albus Dumbledore), Daniel Radcliffe (Harry Potter), and Rupert Grint (Ron Weasley).

Radcliffe acted as spokesman for the group, thanking everyone for attending and praising the theme park design team by saying that he was "grateful that the next part of the Harry Potter legacy has been so well done and well made." The cast then left the platform to chat with children from a San Antonio Texas school who had been selected to be the first Muggles into the Wizarding World of Harry Potter. After briefly chatting with the children, James and Oliver went to an oversized firecracker they had "'found at Zonkers" and after one false start, lit the fuse. Instead of the expected massive display of fireworks there was a small explosion and snow began falling on Hogsmeade. Radcliffe then invited everyone into the park and escorted the school children to an inaugural ride on Flight of the Hippogriff.

Jim Hill related an embarrassing story about Rupert Grint on opening day. Apparently, Grint had been the subject of numerous interviews, "gamely answering the same stupid questions over and over and over again," and autograph signing throughout the morning. After four hours of standing in the heat and guzzling numerous bottles of water, he naturally found he had to use the facilities. He quickly ducked into the restrooms next to the Three Broomsticks.

Meanwhile, hundreds of guests poured into the area and word spread that one of the cast was in the restroom. "So imagine Rupert's surprise when he steps back out into the sunlight and finds that there are now 200+ people waiting for him in the streets. Grint looks out into this veritable sea of digital cameras (which are now recording his every move) and then, right off the top of his head, says: 'Well, I'm really glad that I washed my hands."

It did not take the people at Universal long to realize that the new land was creating staffing problems. Previously, visitors would head to the left and the Marvel Super Hero Island when they first entered Islands of Adventure, but now they turned right, passed through Seuss Landing, often without pausing, and headed straight to Hogsmeade. The result was Universal having "to temporarily shift staff and resources away from Marvel Super Hero Island and Toon Lagoon and then place them over in Seuss Landing, the Lost Continent, and Wizarding World in order to handle the crowds."

Over the next six months Islands of Adventure attendance increased by over 30% largely due to the Wizarding World of Harry Potter. In 2011, the first full year of Wizarding World's operation, there was a further 29% jump in visitors. These figures encouraged Universal to start making plans to expand the park in Orlando and to add Wizarding Worlds to their parks in Japan and Hollywood.

The first anniversary of the opening of Wizarding World of Harry Potter was commemorated at precisely 9:23, the exact time of opening, one year previous, on June 18, 2011. The Hogwarts Express conductor led the countdown and guests and team members were showered with "snow" and golden streamers. Afterwards, complimentary Butterbeer, chocolate frogs, and cauldron cakes were enjoyed by guests. Bill Davis spoke about "creating more exciting memories" for guests "in the years to come."

With the release of *Harry Potter and the Deathly Hallows—Part 2* in July, Universal Orlando representatives magically appeared in all 20 local theaters that were holding a midnight screening of the film and announced that all 3000 attendees would receive complimentary admission to the Wizarding World of Harry Potter. From 3:00 to 5:00 o'clock that morning the guests were given the run of the park to shop in Hogsmeade or tour Hogwarts Castle. As reported by Theme Park Insider, the experience of stepping from the darkened theater after the movie and into the theme park was a "magical and surreal" experience, "just kind of mind-blowing."

The increase in attendance figures over the past year and a half made it abundantly apparent to the powers-that-be at Universal Creative that the way to increase those numbers further was to provide their thousands of guests with even more to get excited about.

Plans to that effect were being drawn up within weeks of the official opening. Mark Woodbury, president of Universal Creative, said, "We knew that there were other great Harry Potter-related tales to tell. That there were stories, characters and experiences that we just hadn't been able to fit into Hogsmeade and Hogwarts Castle." The way to do that was staring people in the face from the moment they walked into Hogsmeade, namely, the Hogwarts Express. "Wouldn't it be great if that train went somewhere?" visitors would exclaim. Woodbury smiled whenever he heard that, for he knew that Universal Creative thought so, too. But where to send it? The obvious answer, partly because it provided more shops for people to spend money in, was London, specifically Diagon Alley. But where to put it?

It was an ambitious and challenging project that would take years and bring together Universal's own magicians from around the globe as they developed new technologies to turn the world of Harry Potter into reality. To understand how they accomplished it, we must go back to when Diagon Alley was just a dirt lot.

Thierry Coup, a senior vice-president of Universal Creative, said: "We are going to create a world that the guests may have seen in a movie, but they only saw a section of it. We'll be able to create all these little alleys, tall urban buildings and have layers and layers of details."

"By placing Diagon Alley and London at Universal Studios Florida and Hogsmeade and Hogwarts at Islands of Adventure," Woodbury speculated, "could we maybe use the distance between these two theme parks as a way to echo the natural geographic separation that the readers find between Hogwarts and Diagon Alley in J.K. Rowling's own stories?"

The idea was unique in theme park construction. It would be like Disneyland offering a way for guests to experience the Pirates of the Caribbean attraction and then sailing over to Disney's California Adventure for an attraction based on *Pirates of the Caribbean: Dead Men Tell No Tales*. To pull off this cinema magic, Universal Creative assembled a team of artists, craftsmen, and creative minds.

When the ideas were presented to Rowling, Woodbury got the impression that "the ambition behind that [idea] was very much appreciated." As steel girders were raised and train track laid, Universal Creative and Warner Bros. "set the bar very high and we weren't about to compromise. We knew that London and Diagon Alley had to be equal to and better than Hogsmeade and Hogwarts Castle in every way and at every level," Woodbury said.

Architecture plays an important part in Hogsmeade/Hogwarts as well as Diagon Alley/London. Authenticity was important to re-create the essence of the books and the transformation from Muggle London to Wizard Diagon Alley. The ride of the Hogwarts Express would not be "the usual theme park thing, where you get on an attraction that promises to take you on a journey, but then when you exit...you're actually back in the exact same spot." Woodbury explained, "After people climb aboard the Hogwarts Express...as they exit that train they're going to find themselves in a completely different place."

Work on the Hogwarts Express/Diagon Alley experience began in June as hundreds of hard-hat wearing workers moved onto the site. The exterior of the London façade was the first project started, as it would shield the rest of the work area from curious Muggles. Work on Diagon Alley would be a masterpiece of illusion, according to Dale Mason, a vice-president of Creative Development: "There's not a real brick in the entire place. Everything...is either modeled fiber glass, steel or carved concrete." The Diagon Alley façades would then be painted and aged to look old. The wizarding world is recognizably stuck in the Victorian era where everything was heated and lit by coal and wood, so there must be lots of soot around as well. At the same time, Steve Jayson's culinary team was working on authentic English dishes for the dining venues under construction. They would present them to Rowling in Edinburgh for her approval.

Work on Hogwarts Express began in England with Universal Creative members spending months there riding the rail systems to get a better feel for what Harry would have experienced. Even the fabric used for the seat cushions on the trains came from the same company that distributed the fabric used in British trains. As Mark Woodbury explained, part of the draw to the new attractions was the attention to detail: "We also created a whole new bunch of fans for the Universal Orlando Resort in the process because we executed Hogsmeade Village and Hogwarts Castle at such a high level."

One of the things Rowling insisted on was that Universal guests have the same experience as Harry when visiting Diagon Alley. Jim Hill explained: "That involves having the back brick wall of this centuries-old pub magically fold in on itself and then reveal this secret wizard shopping district hidden from Muggle eyes right in the middle of London."

In addition to the full-sized re-creation of the Hogwarts Express, the main attraction in the new area would be the coaster-like Harry Potter and the Escape from Gringotts, based on the vaults and dragon sequence from *Harry Potter and the Deathly Hallows—Part 2*. Cast members from the Harry Potter films were thrilled to be reunited and reprise their roles to shoot new scenes for the attraction.

On November 21, 2012, almost two years after filming the final Harry Potter movie and more than two years before Diagon Alley was set to open, actors from the Harry Potter films gathered at Leavesden Studio in Watford, outside of London. Nearly all the original actors were there, including Daniel Radcliffe, Emma Watson, Rupert Grint, Robbie Coltrane, and Helena Bonham Carter, who said: "I forgot how many things could go wrong with the Bellatrix costume," referring to the hanging threads and wild hair.

The actors reminisced about the time spent shooting. Rupert Grint recalled: "We used to say this would be a very good ride with the dragon and the Gringotts vault carts, it's going to be terrifying."

As the actors would be interacting with the audience and not with each other as in the films, shooting was more complex. They had to adjust their thinking of "don't look at the camera" to doing just that.

"It took two years to formalize and to get to a point where we really like the story," said Thierry Coup, who directed the actors on a green screen which would later be merged with graphics to create interactive 3D scenes for the park. They had the advantage of the original film crew being there and they knew all the tricks and techniques used in filming the eight Harry Potter movies.

In December 2012, Coup directed the scenes that would be used in the attraction and said in an interview: "It was obvious that the cast members who came back to be part of the Gringotts shoot really enjoyed the opportunity to revisit these characters." Rowling allowed a certain amount of "creative leeway when it came to Escape From Gringotts," the reason being that the attraction would not be a repeat of the scenes in the film but rather what was happening "concurrently with the events which occurred during *Deathly Hallows*," Coup explained. "Our guests just happen to be at Gringotts Wizarding Bank opening a new account on the exact same day that Harry, Ron, and Hermoine are trying to break into Bellatrix Lestrange's vault to retrieve a horcrux." There is a departure from the original story when Bellatrix and Voldemort arrive to menace the visitors, but Rowling gave her permission to modify the story because the two episodes could possibly have been going on at the same time.

"There's never ever been a theme park attraction...that uses so much cutting-edge technology in the service of telling this one really great story," Thierry said.

Visitors to the park could also enjoy live performances such as a stage show featuring two stories from *The Tales of Beedle the Bard*, or listen to Celestina Warbeck and the Banshees, Molly Weasley's favorite singing group with their renditions of such hits as "You Stole My Cauldron But You Can't Have My Heart" and "You Charmed the Heart Right Out of Me" (both written by J.K. Rowling).

There were also plans for other interactive attractions. The fabled, three-storied Knight Bus from *Harry Potter and the Prisoner of Azkaban* would be parked in London and guests would have an opportunity to chat with the conductor as he carries on a rapport with a shrunken head. At Gringotts Money Exchange, visitors could change their Muggle money into Wizarding World Bank Notes, an idea similar to Disney Dollars but not as elaborate and only in $10 and $20 denominations. Of course, another Ollivander's shop would open in Diagon Alley to match the shop in Hogsmeade.

Tom Williams, chairman and CEO of Universal Parks and Resorts, was intimately involved in what he liked to call "Harry Potter Phase Two." Whenever he could, he'd make his way to the construction site just to walk around and see how things were progressing: "I'm so excited about Potter, I can't see straight. I was out there this morning. I'm out there every day. I'm going to be out there later today. It's just a delight to all your senses in every single respect."

In April 2013, two members of the Universal Creative team flew the almost 5,000 miles to a facility in Switzerland where the Hogwarts Express was being re-created right down to the weathering on the sides of the locomotive. When Diagon Alley was on the drawing boards, Universal Creative needed a way to connect the two sections of park, and they decided on the train as the most logical and most true to the books.

They wanted to re-create the train as seen in the films so they traveled to Great Britain and rode real steam trains, noting all the details that would go into the train in Switzerland.

The prototype is an object of Swiss perfection, but "perfect is a problem when it comes to remaining true to the story," as they wanted the train to look well traveled. Coup recalled: "We had to scratch and dent and really make it feel like it was used. Everything, down to the rivets and the screws and washers and the mahogany panelling that's inside this train, to the fabric on the seats, everything has been researched and authenticated to the highest level."

Dale Mason and Alan Gilmour took Stuart Craig on a tour of the Diagon Alley site in late June 2013 so he could see what had been happening since he was last there. It was a maze of steel and concrete. "There must be a steel shortage in America," Craig remarked.

Universal Creative had been carrying out Craig's vision since they broke ground for the project the previous year. Mark Woodbury stated: "When you arrive in London, its going to be like you arrive in London. This is a real, full-scale environment, King's Cross Station, the Knight Bus will be parked out in front, then you get to go through that wall of London, if you will, and into the actual, magical area of Diagon Alley."

Building in hurricane-prone central Florida presented some unique issues and challenges with building codes. One of the biggest challenges was to build the structures to look aged, but to conceal sophisticated technology and design. With safety as the top priority, more structure and detail was necessary.

Gringotts Bank was a ride waiting to happen and it would be the central draw when a 64-foot fire breathing dragon was mounted on top. Constructing the vault under the bank was no small effort, requiring 37,411 square feet of sculpted stone with concrete sprayed onto it. Kings Cross was to have the dimensions of a real station.

"There are millions of huge problems, nobody knows how they are going to be fixed and they dive in and just work it out as they go along," Craig explained. "The goal is authenticity and the bar is set very high," Coup added. "We took two weeks working out how dirty the rubbish bins should be."

New music was recorded at Abbey Road Studios in London by the London Symphony orchestra in March 2014. The same musicians who recorded the musical score for the films were now "recording a whole new arrangement for our new attractions," both the train ride and Escape from Gringotts.

Gilmour and Coup gave Bonnie Wright (Ginny Wealsey), James Phelps (Fred Weasley), and Oliver Phelps (George Weasley) a tour of the Hogwarts Express attraction prior to opening day. Upon seeing a scene out the window with George and Fred Weasley on their brooms, James quipped, "I took one take, he took about ten." After riding the Hogwarts Express, they wandered the streets, toured Weasley's Wizard Wheezes, dined at the Three Broomsticks, strolled through Gringotts and tried Butterbeer ice cream at Fortescue's Ice Cream Parlour.

"It doesn't feel like a replica or interpretation of what we had it was...what we had," Bonnie Wright later reported.

As the park neared completion, rehearsals were intensified for Shaullanda Lacombe (Celestina Warbick) and her backup singers (the Banshees) and the actors for *Tales of Beedle the Bard*.

Hundreds of positions needed to be filled ahead of the impending opening. An open house job fair was held at CityWalk and a new pay scale went into effect that was calculated to move Universal ahead of Walt Disney World. On June 1, Universal raised its starting wage from $8 to $9 per hour. In addition, 3,500 new employees were required, full time, part time, and seasonal, not only for the new Diagon Alley area, but also the eight new CityWalk venues and Universal's Cabana Beach Resort Hotel.

Butterbeer is the main piece of magic that Universal surveys show that guests wish they could take home. This is not surprising, as Chef Steven Jayson, vice president and corporate executive chef for Universal Parks & Resorts, and his team labored off and on for nearly three years to come up with a workable real-world recipe for this magical, mythical brew. Although Butterbeer is frequently mentioned in the books and films, no recipe was ever divulged.

When it came time to make it available in the new Wizarding World park, something had to be available for the discerning Potterphile. Jayson and his team went to work to create a beverage that would satisfy not only the average visitor, but especially J.K. Rowling. In 2008, Jayson consulted with Rowling in Scotland on how best to flavor the imaginary drink, as they could find few references in the books other than it can give the drinker a bit of a buzz. House elves were particularly susceptible to the effects of Butterbeer and Winky often got herself drunk on it, requiring Dobby to take her to the Room of Requirement to find an antidote to sober her up.

Universal wanted as many people to be able to drink Butterbeer as possible, including the lactose intolerant, so there could be not butter or other dairy products. Rowling agreed, but insisted that Butterbeer be made with real sugar as she was against using corn syrup, a trans-fat.

With this information in mind, Jayson and his team sequestered themselves in the Universal kitchens and got to work. It has been reported that the Butterbeer team spent three or four months and made 15 or 16 attempts before Jayson was satisfied that they had perfected the beverage. He recalled in a 2010 interview: "This was a pretty daunting situation. We knew that people's expectations were going to be very high. What's more, we had to create a beverage that was good for all ages. We experimented with all sorts of flavors. It took awhile to get the flavor right where it needed to be. So it wasn't too sweet. That it had this great comfortable feeling going down."

Now satisfied with his creation, and getting the okay from his Universal bosses, Jayson presented his drink to Rowling for her final approval. Mark Woodbury, head of Universal Creative, jokingly recalled: "[It] was something of a challenge, getting all of that stuff past the Department of Homeland Security." Once in Edinburgh, Jayson whipped up four variations of Butterbeer in rented space in a hotel kitchen, including the variation that the Universal executives hoped she would pick. Universal's senior vice president in charge of Food & Beverages, Richard Florell, carried that tray of drinks to Rowling. She sampled each of the beverages and when she was done selected the one that Jayson and the Universal executives had preferred, saying, "Yes, Chef. That's it."

Now all that was left to do was satisfy the public. They realized they had done just that when the line for the Butterbeer cart was sometimes as long as the queue for the attractions. Butterbeer has been the most sought after beverage in Islands of Adventure. The one-millionth mug was sold in January 2011, less than seven months after it first went on sale in the Wizarding World. On December 12, 2012, Universal celebrated the sale of its five-millionth cup of Butterbeer. Do a little math and that equates to 5,500 Butterbeers a day since opening. This doesn't include the free Butterbeer given to everyone from the twenty-foot Butterbeer barrel cart in the Wizarding World on its first anniversary.

The exact ingredients are unknown, but when the beverage is being poured for the guests a mixture of what tastes like butterscotch, shortbread, and cream soda is poured in first, followed by a lighter, fluffier version to form the head. The beverage is prepared on site and, according to Chef Jayson, Universal has "implanted special security procedures to protect the recipe."

Soft openings were held for families of Universal employees that were invariably hosted by Harry Potter cast members. Robbie Coltrane (Rubeus Hagrid), with the help of a pink umbrella, walked on stage to announce, "Welcome, welcome everybody to Diagon Alley," followed by fireworks over Kings Cross Station.

Wizarding World of Harry Potter—Diagon Alley opened on July 8, 2014. As with the previous opening of Wizarding World of Harry Potter—Hogsmeade, there was a plethora of film stars from the Harry Potter movies as well as Universal executives. The usual speech making and fireworks was followed by hordes of Potterphiles making their excited way into the park.

CHAPTER FIVE

INSIDE THE WIZARDING WORLD—HOGSMEADE

Since opening day there have been two ways to enter the Wizarding World of Harry Potter at Islands of Adventure in Universal Studios Orlando. Visitors must first pass through the entrance to the park at Port of Entry, turn right and walk through Seuss Landing, then enter the Lost Continent and proceed until coming to the entrance of Hogsmeade. Another route, which is much less visually impressive and more circuitous, is through the back door via Jurassic Park, which leads into Wizarding World at the opposite end of Hogsmeade.

The portal through which visitors pass from the Lost Continent side is a stone block archway with a black, metal sign hanging from the center. The sign has a large boar cut out of it with the words "Please respect the Spell Limits" beneath. Above the boar is a silhouette of Hogsmeade. The entranceway is meant to represent Hogsmeade Station where students first disembark from Hogwarts Express.

In the books and films, Hogsmeade Station is the arrival and departure point for Hogwarts students on their way to or from the venerable old school. Hogsmeade Village was founded over a thousand years ago by a medieval wizard named Hengist of Woodcroft. He stopped there as he was fleeing persecution by Muggles around the same time as Hogwarts School of Witchcraft and Wizardry was founded.

The scenes of Hogsmade Station in *Harry Potter and the Philosopher's (Sorcerer's) Stone* were shot at Goathland village station, a heritage line run by North Yorkshire Moors Railway, that most resembles the park entrance. The second appearance of the station in *Harry Potter and the Order of the Phoenix* was shot at a re-created site in Black Park where most of the Forbidden Forest scenes were also shot.

When this area of the park first opened, there was a replica of the Hogwarts Express parked near the entrance to Hogsmeade quietly belching steam. Nearby was an attendant conductor ready to answer questions and make certain that no overly enthusiastic children (or adults) attempted to climb on the locomotive. While speaking to this gentleman, visitors would probably notice he had an English accent. In many cases. Universal hired Britons to work in the Wizarding World. Also, new hires for the area had to well versed in the lore of the Harry Potter books and movies so that any interactions with guests would be authentic.

The village laid out before visitors is rendered in superb detail. The shops and cottages with their steep, snow-covered slate roofs and multi-paned, bowed windows looking out into the street invite guests in with their displays of magical things. The buildings are covered in granite from the Scottish mountains in which the village is supposed to be nestled. Crow-step gables; tall, crooked chimneys; and wee dormer windows are typical of 17th century Scottish architecture.

To the right after passing under the arch is the first ride, Dragon Challenge. Originally known as Dueling Dragons, it was modified to fit the Harry Potter theme. The queue was rethemed in late 2009 and the ride closed later for the refurbishment of the attraction itself. When the park officially opened on June 18, 2010, the ride had been renamed Dragon Challenge and based on a sequence from *Harry Potter and the Goblet of Fire*.

Guests enter the queue and pass by numerous Triwizard Tournament banners representing the four contestants. Inexplicably (as the car only appeared in *Harry Potter and the Chamber of Secrets*), the Weasley's crashed Ford Anglia is seen just before guests enter the Champion's tent and pass the legendary, glowing Triwizard Cup. Guests now must choose whether they want to ride the Hungarian Horntail (on the right) or the Chinese Fireball dragon (on the left).

The Hungarian Horntail was the dragon that Harry selected to battle as the first task of the Triwizard Tournament. The

Hungarian Horntail in *Harry Potter and the Goblet of Fire* had "evil, yellow eyes...a monstrous, scaly black lizard, thrashing her spiked tail," quite different from the dragon depicted in the film. The Chinese Fireball was selected by Drumstrang Academy champion Viktor Krum. This dragon was described as "a red one with an odd fringe of fine gold spikes around its face...shooting mushroom-shaped fire clouds."

Dragon Challenge is an intertwined, inverted roller coaster designed by Switzerland's Bollinger and Mabillard. The steel and fiberglass trains consist of eight cars, each with four seats, to accommodate 32 passengers at one time. The ride is unique to the Orlando park.

The Hungarian Horntail (on a blue track) could reach speeds of 55 mph while the Chinese Fireball (on a red track) sped up to 60 mph along a 3,200-foot steel track featuring five inversions. The two dragons traverse different courses involving an initial 125-foot climb, followed by sharp drops, loops, and corkscrews. In the original version, Dueling Dragons, the trains were launched simultaneously and on three occasions during the 2-minute and 25-second ride seemed to charge at and barely miss each other. After a couple of injuries were sustained due to loose items from one dragon striking passengers in the other, the coasters were shut down until an investigation was completed. When the attraction reopened the near-miss aspect was eliminated, with the coasters now dispatched separately. There have been no injuries reported since the change was made.

The second ride in Hogsmeade, Flight of the Hippogriff, is billed by Universal as a "training flight" on "an enchanting family coaster woven from wicker and decorated with fluttering leaves representing feathers." Based on scenes from *Harry Potter and the Prisoner of Azkaban*, the ride is situated at the opposite end of Hogsmeade from Dragon Challenge and next to Hogwarts Castle. Flight of the Hippogriff was rethemed from an earlier ride known as the Flying Unicorn.

Visitors approach the ride along a pathway that begins with stone pillars and passes by Hagrid's Hut, from which the barking of Hagrid's boarhound, Fang, can be heard. The hut is based on the newer, expanded version from *Harry*

Potter and the Prisoner of Azkaban. Here, Rubeus Hagrid, the gamekeeper and newly minted professor (voiced by Robbie Coltrane), is teaching his first Care of Magical Creatures class. Note the crate outside the front door labeled "Baby Norwegian Ridgeback," which was used to ship the baby dragon Norbert to Romania. Before getting on the ride, passengers are taught how to properly approach a hippogriff, slowly, with head bowed. If the hippogriff bows back, it is safe to approach it. Visitors then board the cars in a covered area and set off, passing Buckbeak the hippogriff, who bows.

The animatronic hippogriff is based on the model made for filming the creature as it sat in Hagrid's pumpkin patch awaiting its fate in *Harry Potter and the Prisoner of Azkaban*. The train consists of a wicker-headed hippogriff followed by nine, two-passenger wicker cars. The ride lasts for about a minute, but the views of Hagrid's Hut, Hogsmeade, Hogwarts Castle, and the chance to meet Buckbeak are worth it.

The third and most spectacular attraction in Hogsmeade is the dark ride Harry Potter and the Forbidden Journey, housed within Hogwarts Castle. When visitors first arrive in Hogsmeade they can only see the top of the castle, but as they progress into the town, the castle draws them in until they can see the structure in its entirety. This is a technique Walt Disney used in Disneyland building Sleeping Beauty Castle at the end of Main Street to act as a "wienie" (Walt's term) to entice guests into his park. Compared to the castle in the films, Universal's is much smaller but the main identifying features—the Great Hall, the Astronomy Tower, the courtyard, and the staircase tower—are all represented.

Forced perspective makes the building appear larger than it is: as the scale decreases, the higher up the structure goes. Unfortunately, there are unavoidable design flaws as parts, of the show building can be seen behind Flight of the Hippogriff. Despite Universal Creative's efforts, the enormous building could not be completely camouflaged due to the existence of a service road behind the Hippogriff's ride and the huge size of the structure.

The vehicle in which visitors view Harry Potter and the Forbidden Journey is known as an "enchanted bench," a single row of four seats attached to a robotic arm manufactured by Keller und Knappich Augsburg (KUKA) Robotics Corporation. Initially designed for use in automobile manufacture, KUKA later adapted the arm for amusement park use as what has been termed a robocoaster. In fact, it has no resemblance to a true coaster. Similar uses for the KUKA system are used in Sum of all Thrills in Walt Disney World's Epcot and Knight's Tournament in Legoland California. Harry Potter and the Forbidden Journey differs from those two by being a tracked version of the system that only uses a single ride profile.

Using a continuous loading system, the benches never stop as guests board from a moving platform belt similar to that used in Disney's Haunted Mansion and other Omnimover attractions. The sweeping motion of the robotic arm gives the rider the sensation of increasing and decreasing speed, though the vehicle never does so. The arm also points the visitor in the direction of the action being shown on the screens before them. Unlike other rides of this type, animatronics and set pieces are used to enhance the experience. Figures such as the Sorting Hat, Whomping Willow, a dragon, spiders, and some of the Dementors are animatronic, with the visuals transitioning between screen and animatronics as the screens follow the benches. Some special effects enhance the experience as spiders spit on the riders and the dragon exhales a steamy breath.

To many Potterphiles, the queue leading into Hogwarts and eventually the Forbidden Journey attraction is almost as exciting as the ride itself. The experience begins as they pass between the two stone pillars of the gates of Hogwarts, topped by winged boars. On the face of the pillars is the Hogwarts crest and the school name. By using fiber optics, the words Harry Potter and the Forbidden Journey appear every few seconds in script on the pillars.

A set of test seats is positioned nearby to ascertain the eligibility of guests to ride. These seats have been updated since they were first installed to allow oversized guests to ride, something not possible in the early days of the attraction. Lockers are provided for those who wish to stow their belongings as the seats are not equipped for guests to carry large items.

The queue then winds into a dimly lit dungeon-like room where single riders and standby guests go their separate ways. As guests proceed they come upon artifacts from the films between the Mirror of Erised and the statue of the One-Eyed Witch. Farther on is the door to the Potions Classroom from behind which a female professor can be heard as she gives her class a lecture. Leaving the hallway, guests find themselves back outside and entering the Hogwarts Greenhouse where the bulk of the queue is contained in several undercover switchbacks, the number of which depends on the length of the queue. There is little to see here beyond a display of stationary mandrakes and the superb work done by Universal Creative to age the greenhouse area.

Guests now re-enter the castle to find a statue of the unnamed Hogwarts architect and nearby four hourglasses displaying the House Points. Gryffindor is winning. The next statue is of the first Hogwarts headmaster, name unknown, followed soon after by the gold Griffin statue that is the entrance to the elevator to Headmaster Albus Dumbledore's office. The password must have been changed as the words "sherbet lemon" used in the films do not activate the entrance.

After meandering down a few short corridors, guests pass a large tapestry depicting a unicorn (a 16th century Dutch work known as *Unicorn in Captivity*) and down another hallway to two more paintings. The first is of Professor Swoopstick who describes and intricacies of the game of Quidditch then leaves his portrait to appear in the other picture, which depicts spectators watching a Quidditch match, to continue his narrative. This area leads into a large portrait gallery with several paintings. Of these, the four depicting the Hogwarts founders, Godric Gryffindor, Helga Hufflepuff, Rowena Ravenclaw, and Salazar Slytherin, are animated and carry on a spirited conversation with each other. The "paintings" are essentially television screens with picture frames around them.

Dumbledore's office is the next scene guests enter as they pass by cabinets filled with wizard books, telescopes, and the Pensieve. Beyond can be seen Dumbledore's desk and the headmaster himself, standing high above on a balcony. He welcomes the visitors and gives a brief history of the school and a warning about meeting "all manner of things not common to your own world: ghosts, house elves, giants, and apparently, as of this morning, a dragon." After a few words of advice about making "a choice between what is right and what is easy," he explains that being without a Defence Against the Dark Arts teacher, a lecture by Professor Binns on Hogwarts Through the Centuries will follow. (There are two slightly different versions of Dumbledore's speech just as there are two versions of the earlier exchange between the Hogwarts founders.)

Guests now proceed into the Defence Against the Dark Arts classroom with its chalkboard of spells, dragon skeleton suspended from the ceiling, and staircase to the DADA professor's office. Voices can be heard as the door to the office opens and Harry Potter, Ron Weasley, and Hermione Granger appear from under an invisibility cloak. They are here to help as Ron explains: "We thought some of you might be looking for a way to escape Professor Binns' lecture. If you're not, you're mental." Harry adds that he thought a game of Quidditch would be more interesting, after which Hermione offers to sneak them out of the castle, saying: "All you have to do is follow me to the Room of Requirement, and I'll manage it from there." (There are two versions of this exchange.) The technology used for Dumbledore and later Harry, Ron, and Hermione to speak to guests is a "Musion effect" attained by projecting the film onto glass.

On their way to the Room of Requirement as suggested by Hermione, visitors arrive at the portrait of the Fat Lady who has instructions to let them into the Gryffindor Common Room without a password. In the Common Room is a fireplace, chairs, various props scattered about, and a stairway to the bedrooms above. There are also three portraits which argue about the best way to use the enchanted benches which Hermione has cast a flying spell on and where the Muggles are about to sit. This is also an opportunity for those who only wanted to take the castle tour to exit the queue, something permitted but not encouraged by staff.

Three lines are formed and guests proceed down their corridor toward the Sorting Hat, which is giving a safety spiel, and a Hogwarts student instructing guests when to board. They have now entered the Room of Requirement. Overhead candles are floating and a continuous glide of benches passes, facing visitors, with the robotic arm in the rear. Once guests have found their vehicle they pull down the over-the-shoulder restraint and travel along for a time beside a series of mirrors until they see Hermione on a balcony with some floo powder. "Alright, say 'Observatory,'" she says, "on three. One, two, three!"

The floo powder ignites in a blast of green smoke and guests are hurled through a series of chimneys and emerge in the Observatory with a view from high above Hogwarts. The bench slips through the astronomy clock window and speeds around the Hogwarts grounds. Harry and Ron appear on their brooms to guide the bench to the Quidditch pitch. Hagrid is standing on a bridge as they approach and asks, "Hey, you lot! Haven't seen a dragon, have ye?"

No sooner has he asked when a dragon appears, swoops toward Harry, then perches on the other side of the bridge as the bench careens in that direction. The dragon pursues as the bench maneuvers around the burn mark-scarred bridge. An escape is found, but the floor drops out and the guests are face to face with the fiery breath of the dragon which blasts them into the Forbidden Forest.

(At one point while the attraction was being designed there was to be a Dementors and Voldemort scene between the dragon attack and the Forbidden Forest sequence; apparently, this was never used.)

Having escaped the dragon by entering the dark and spooky forest, lightning flashes disclose an army of spiders now surrounding the bench. Turning to escape, visitors come face to face with the acromantula, Aragog. Hermione appears and casts a spider dispersing spell as the bench moves to face another wall of spiders. In the darkness that follows riders are sprayed with spider venom as Hermione urges them to "Hurry on to the Quidditch pitch, and watch out for the Whomping Willow!" Just then the huge tree swats a branch at the bench. It misses with the first swing, but the second time the bench is knocked to the Quidditch pitch.

There is a fast and furious match between Gryffindor and Slytherin in progress. Harry is in pursuit of the Golden Snitch when Draco Malfoy rams into him. Ron blocks a shot at goal, then points and shouts "Dementors!" Harry leads the bench away from the group of Dementors, but one of them grabs him as he and the bench dive into a cave leading to the Chamber of Secrets.

In the darkness a huge animatronic Dementor looms over the bench which attempts to flee but runs into another of the fiends. To escape, the bench flies through the chamber, passing the basilisk skeleton and into the cave where the statue head of Salazar Slytherin still sits. They are unable to avoid the Dementor and the four visitors are locked in a Dementor's Kiss. Harry arrives and casts the Expecto Patronum charm which fends off the Dementor, but also causes the cave to start to collapse.

Harry tells the bench to follow him as rocks begin to fall all around them. Dodging the rocks, the bench manages to get safely out of the cave, speed over the Black Lake, barely miss a flock of birds, and circle around Hogwarts, passing the Great Hall where Harry is being congratulated for saving the bench-riding Muggles. Dumbledore and other students are seen just before the bench re-enters the Floo Network through a haze of green and comes to rest back in the Room of Requirement.

Exiting the attraction visitors descend into Filch's Emporium of Confiscated Goods, one of the few shops created specifically for the Wizarding World that does not appear in any of the books or films. Here guests can select from the many merchandise items available which Argus Filtch had supposedly confiscated from students over the years of his tenure as caretaker of Hogwarts, such as Hogwarts house scarfs, house crest pins, leather journals, Golden Snitches, Marauders' Maps, omnioculars, and other toys and souvenirs. Replicas of film props are also available, including chess sets, walking sticks, and death-eater masks. Guests can also buy the photographs taken of them on the ride. A few items used in the Harry Potter films are on display, like a Whack Trance Whammy Rocket, Filch's Secrecy Sensor, a Fanged Flyer, a bottle of Skele-gro, and a Crystal Incantation Comet.

There are several other shops in Hogsmeade where Harry Potter merchandise can be purchased. Perhaps the most famous of these is Ollivanders, "makers of fine wands since 382

B.C." According to the books and films, the main Ollivanders store was located in Diagon Alley on the south side of London and owned by the Ollivander family, the best wandmakers in Britain. Harry Potter visited the store to obtain his wand prior to his first year at Hogwarts. The shop was described as narrow and shabby with peeling gold letters over the door. There was also a branch of Ollivanders on High Street in Hogsmeade run by an associate of Garrick Ollivander.

The shop contains "countless wand boxes stacked to the ceiling" and a unique interactive experience where a wand choses a wizard. Guests can purchase their own wand, a collectible wand set, or choose from a selection of film character wands.

One of the more popular, though expensive, products of the Wizarding World is the interactive wand. These important wizard implements come with a map showing spell casting locations throughout the Wizarding World. As the concept was introduced later in the area's history, spells are more complex and frequent in Diagon Alley than in Hogsmeade. Some of the latter are repurposed effects that formerly worked by themselves.

Dogweed and Deathcap is the façade of a shop that sells exotic plants and flowers, presumably including dogweed and deathcap. The interactive wand will cause flowers to grow in the pot in the window.

In the books and films, Dervish and Banges is a wizarding equipment shop located near the end of High Street in Hogsmeade. Here magical equipment is sold and repaired. There is a path nearby that leads to a cave that Sirius Black used as a hideout in book *Harry Potter and the Prisoner of Azkaban*. In the Wizarding World version, a number of magical items such as omnioculars, sneakoscopes, spectrespecs, and the *Monster Book of Monsters* are available. Quidditch supplies are also obtainable, including quaffles, snitches, and brooms, even the Firebolt or Nimbus 2001. Clothing, from t-shirts to ties, scarfs, and robes can also be purchased here. When an interactive wand is used, a small dragon will fly around the Hogwarts in the window, pursuing a miniature Harry Potter on a broom.

At the façade for Dominic Maestro's Music Shop is the enchanted cello in a second-story window. Whenever it hits a sour note, there is a flurry in the sheet music.

For those with a sweet tooth there is Honeydukes. In the books and films the store is operated by Ambrosius Flume and his wife and is in the village of Hogsmeade. "There were shelves upon shelves of the most succulent-looking sweets imaginable." First established in 1641, this legendary wizard's sweet shop is frequented by students and teachers alike. There is a secret passageway from Hogwarts School to Honeydukes which is accessed from a large statue of Gunhilda of Gorsemoor on the third floor of the castle. The narrow, low, earthy passage takes an hour or so to traverse and ends at a long stone staircase which leads into the cellar of Honeydukes through an impossible-to-see trapdoor in the floor. Like the original, the Wizarding World version sells Acid Pops, Bertie Bott's Every Flavour Beans, Cauldron Cakes, Exploding Bonbons, Fizzing Whizzbees, Chocolate Frogs with lenticular wizard cards, and other delicious treats. The interactive wand will open a box of croaking chocolate frogs in a front window.

McHavelock's Wizarding Headgear is a wizarding shop that specializes in hats and wigs in Hogsmeade. The interactive wand will bring to life a pair of pixies in a cauldron above the façade. Tomes and Scrolls is a specialist bookshop established in 1768. There is a sign above McHavelocks and the interactive wand opens a copy of the *Tales of Beedle the Bard* in the front window.

The Owl Post Office in Hogsmeade is the equivalent to a Muggle post office, but with owls delivering the letters. The owls are color-coded for short distances, long distances, and for speed of delivery. The Owl Post Office is used by wizards who do not have their own owls or access to one. Newspapers, personal letters, and packages can all be delivered by owl. The Owl Post Office is said to have a putrid smell equivalent to a dung bomb. The Wizarding World version has animatronic owls perched in the timber rafters and on the walls, but they do not actually deliver the mail; that is left up to the Muggle letter carriers. There is a post box available for letters and postcards that will receive a Hogsmeade postmark. There are also

Wizarding World stamps that can be purchased to mail those letters. A variety of stationery, writing implements (including quills), and owl-related gifts are available for sale. Next to the Owl Post Office, in a storefront window, a holographic howler will yell at you for not having your permission slip. The red envelope will rip itself up once the message is delivered.

Next to the Owl Post Office and across the street from the Three Broomsticks is the Owlery where a shaded area provides a place for visitors to relax and cool down on hot Florida summer days. Inside, animatronic owls hoot and move their heads about from the rafters where one can also find simulated owl droppings.

Spintwitches Sporting Needs is a shop that sells sporting goods and Quidditch supplies. In the front window façade is a Quidditch case that the interactive wand will cause the quaffle and bludger to attempt to vacate. There is also a runaway Snitch flitting around inside the window.

To keep the village in tune with its depiction in the films, some of the shops are of necessity quite small, seldom able to comfortably accommodate more that 20 people at a time. This creates a phenomenon seldom seen in theme parks wherein the lines for the shops are often longer than the queues for the attractions. One exception is Honeydukes which has more overall space but narrow aisles to display all the goodies. To satisfy Potterphiles' need for merchandise, street vendors and Port of Entry shops also stock wizard products.

Next to Honeydukes was Zonko's Joke Shop, a favorite place for Hogwarts students to shop as it was the purveyor of "jokes and tricks to fulfil even Fred and George Weasley's wildest dreams." These included Dungbombs, Hiccough Sweets, Frog Spawn Soap, Sugar Quills, and Nose-biting Teacups. Zonko's storefront has been switched out as the products within prepared for a move to Diagon Alley's Weasley's Wizard Wheezes. Zonko's closing in 2014 made room for an expansion of Honeydukes next door.

Before the Wizarding World Diagon Alley expansion, Wiseacre's Wizarding Equipment was a façade in Hogsmeade that was renamed Madam Puddifoot's Tea Shop. The new tea spot, though still a façade, will be familiar to those who remember Harry and Cho Chang's Valentine's Day date in *Harry Potter and the Goblet of Fire*. There is a snowman cake topper in the window that will skate around if an interactive wand is used.

If all these attractions and shops have made guests hungry, then the place for them to go is the Three Broomsticks. This rustic tavern has buffeteria service for all meals. *Harry Potter and the Half-Blood Prince* was being filmed while the Wizarding World was being designed and constructed, so it is suspected that the Three Broomsticks set was based on the one being built in the park rather than the reverse, as was true of all other sets. The Three Broomsticks and the neighboring Hog's Head Pub were once the popular Enchanted Oak Tavern of the Lost Continent. The conversion to Potter use greatly reduced seating capacity and at peak times 30 minute waits are not uncommon.

The refurbishing of the tavern included adding weathered open beams, balconies, vaulted ceiling, cast iron chandeliers, antlers around a huge fireplace, and incredible detail that enabled the designers to completely disguise any signs of Muggle technology.

In the books and films, the Three Broomsticks is a popular inn and pub, allegedly as old as Hogsmeade itself and frequented by students and teachers from Hogwarts School. Owned and operated by Madam Rosmerta, the warm, crowded, and often smoky inn is clean and welcoming. Butterbeer and Firewhiskey are served along with mulled mead, red currant run, gillywater, cherry syrup, and soda.

The Wizarding World version is a buffeteria-style restaurant serving fish and chips, Cornish pastry, soup, salads, shepherd's pie, apple pie, and chocolate trifle, all washed down with Pumpkin Juice or Butterbeer. There is also a children's menu with macaroni and cheese, chicken fingers, fish and chips with pie, and ice cream or trifle for dessert. What you won't find is food that does not fit the British theme of the park. No chicken nuggets or hot dogs here; even Coca-Cola, Universal's soft drink partner, is not sold in the Wizarding World.

For those who prefer beer, spirits, or wine, the Hog's Head pub is to the rear of the Three Broomsticks. The Hog's Head brew is exclusive to Universal. Younger Muggles can drink Butterbeer or Pumpkin Juice. A large stuffed hog's head on the wall behind the bar periodically snarls at guests, and the fireplace has wizard's names carved over it.

Unlike the cozier, friendly Three Broomsticks, in the books and films the Hog's Head Inn is small, dirty, and dingy. The windows are so dirty they cannot be seen through; the floor, though made of stone, appears to be a dirt floor and the tables are made of rough wood with a single candle for light. Aberforth Dumbledore is the owner and operator of this disreputable establishment and was not pleased when the room filed up with students seeking to establish Dumbledore's Army in *Harry Potter and the Order of the Phoenix*. During the Second Wizarding War, the Hog's Head and Hogwarts' Room of Requirement were connected by a tunnel providing safe access for the members of the revised Dumbeldore's Army in *Harry Potter and the Deathly Hallows*.

When using the bathrooms in Hogsmeade, guests of both genders often hear the ghostly crying and whining of Moaning Myrtle. Though usually restricted to the first-floor bathroom in Hogwarts, the young Ravenclaw ghost apparently likes to move about when the castle is too quiet.

To entertain guests as they stroll the streets or wait in lines, the Frog Choir steps up and puts on a ten-minute show reminiscent of the Hogwarts choir directed by Professor Flitwick in *Harry Potter and the Prisoner of Azkaban*. There are four singers in the choir, two of whom hold large frogs sitting on pillows. Their repertoire consists of a few wizard-related songs including "Hedwig's Theme" and "Something Wicked This Way Comes."

In the same venue, an alcove between Flight of the Hippogriff and Dragon Challenge, the Triwizard Spirit Rally is held. This show features three men in Durmstrang Institute uniforms performing martial arts moves and four women from Beauxbatons Academy in pale blue dresses displaying their talents at simple rhythmic gymnastics with ribbons. The routines are similar to those displayed as the competing schools are introduced during *Harry Potter and the Goblet of Fire*. After the six-minute show, the dancers are available for photos ops.

At this time the future of Wizarding World of Harry Potter—Hogsmeade is, once again, fueled primarily by rumours. In March 2017, *Orlando Business Journal* reported on a conversation with "an insider" from Universal who stated: "Universal and Warner Bros. are working on a replacement for Dragon Challenge." Since it "wasn't built as an original Potter attraction, it makes sense to change it out." The source added: "From what I was told, it may have a portion as if you are in a forest, with part of the ride outside, and other parts indoor designed to make you feel like you're outside. It sounded more like a dark ride."

The project has not been confirmed by Universal and the possibility of a *Fantastic Beasts and Where to Find Them* tie-in has also been rumoured with a possible 2020 opening date. Warner Bros. confirmed that there would be a *Fantastic Beasts* tie-in to the theme parks when the films were announced in 2012.

CHAPTER SIX

INSIDE THE WIZARDING WORLD—DIAGON ALLEY

The first hint that something big was scheduled to happen began with the closing of the Jaws attraction at Universal Studios in Florida. The removal of the popular attraction was announced on December 2, 2012, and one month later the final ride wended its way through the water course. By the following morning the entire Amity Harbor area had been walled off and demolition began, continuing over the ensuing months. All that remains of the Jaws attraction today is the hanging shark vignette which was relocated to the Fisherman's Wharf area of the San Francisco section of the park.

Rumors began to fly after the announcement. Speculation ranged from Transformers to Family Guy attractions. It would be over a year before Universal Orlando announced on May 8, 2013, that the new area would be the Wizarding World of Harry Potter—Diagon Alley. The announcement served to fuel rumors rather than quell them as only a single piece of concept art was released at the time. Thierry Coup, senior vice president of Universal Creative and executive creative director for the Wizarding World of Harry Potter—Diagon Alley, said of the artwork: "The illustration is obviously an illustration. It's an artist's depiction of what the experience will feel like, but the level of detail that's in this rendering is not true to the real thing. It's going to be so much higher in details."

He shed more light on the project in a subsequent interview: "We brought Hogsmeade Village and Hogwarts to life back in 2010, but for us, and listening to our guests and fans, to complete the whole story of the Harry Potter fiction it really also had to be Diagon Alley and London and the Hogwarts Express and Gringotts Bank—all the other elements that were part of Harry Potter's life and his beginning into the world of being a wizard.

"When we tried to place Diagon right next to Hogsmeade, we quickly realized you can't just walk from Scotland to London. You can't see London facades right next to Hogwarts. Jaws offered the largest area for us to create something that was about the same footprint that we did back at Hogsmeade. Jaws had been here for about 22 years and it was still going well. But in the rating of all the attractions of the park, it was probably time for it to be refreshed or changed."

The former Jaws attraction area proved to be perfect for the Dagon Alley project, as it was located in a remote corner of the park and therefore conducive to the creation of a totally self-contained area. There would be no outside distractions while guests were in the Wizarding World. No sooner had the demolition of Jaws been completed than work began on Diagon Alley. Universal was not wasting time capitalizing on the hype surrounding the debut of what is now known as Wizarding World of Harry Potter—Hogsmeade. No firm dates were divulged for the opening other than some time in 2014.

With the majority of guests now flocking to Islands of Adventure, Universal had to find a way to keep attendance balanced between the two parks. Early on in the development of the Wizarding World, Universal Creative had planned to attach Diagon Alley to Hogsmeade within Islands of Adventure. However, it did not seem to be in keeping with Rowling's vision to have one visible from the other. Mark Woodbury decided it would be best to build Diagon Alley in Universal Studios Florida and connect it to Islands of Adventure with the Hogwarts Express transporting guests from one park to the other through Universal's backstage area. Visual and special effects would be used so that none of that would be seen from the train. As the parks are separate entities, some sort of park-to-park ticket system was also in the works.

The train would leave from a Muggle London façade featuring a row of buildings that exist in the real world, including King's Cross Station. Each of the façades "played a part in

Harry Potter stories and the films." Coup explained. The Knight Bus, which had been part of the grand opening of the Hogsmeade portion of the park in 2010, would become a permanent part of the Diagon Alley extension.

No details were released at the time, but there were plans to incorporate Platform 9¾ into the experience. Nor would Universal release details for what shops or restaurants would be replicated. Coup stated: "I can't really say all the details of these places, but certainly all the signature places will be part of this and some additional ones that may not have appeared in the films, but were certainly part of the stories."

It was pointed out that the Hogsmede area already had an Ollivander's, but in the books and films, that establishment had been located in Diagon Alley. Apparently, this inconsistency was permitted by Rowling. Coup said: "J.K. Rowling gave us the okay to open an annex to Ollivanders, which was in Hogsmeade Village." Another Ollivanders was likely in Diagon Alley, though wasn't confirmed at the time.

The Diagon Alley area was designed to have a similar footprint to Hogsmeade, though the Hogwarts Express connection would expand upon that. As with Hogsmeade, Rowling had input but left more creative control in the hands of Universal Creative. Coup explained: "She's been partnering with us in the development, in the conceptualization of this to ensure that it is true and authentic." The Warner Bros. film production team of Stuart Craig and Alan Gilmore were also working closely with the designers to assure that every detail is true to the films. "If we'd have filmed the movie here, we'd all have been a lot better. You can't help but get brought into the role," Matthew Lewis (Neville Longbottom) stated.

Attention to detail was of major importance in the making of Diagon Alley. Universal Creative's senior props manager, Eric Baker, and his team spent three years seeking unique items to display. In addition to antique stores and flea markets, they had access to Warner Bros. warehouses for set dressings and props used in the films. They used molds of many of the props to create exact replicas. "We were able to take things from the movies and make them live on forever for everyone that visits the park," Baker stated.

Andy Brennan, industry analyst with IBISWorld, remarked: "Hogsmeade reportedly cost over $250 million" and Diagon Alley cost about $400 million to build. Brennan estimated that "combined attendance at Islands of Adventure and Universal Studios has jumped more than 50% since 2009. NBCUniversal's theme park revenue is up nearly 40% since 2009, much of which can be directly attributed to the popular WWHP." According to VisitOrlando.com, there were 59 million visitors in 2013, up 27% from 46.6 million in 2009.

In an unprecedented move, Universal Orlando invited a group of media people on a private tour of the construction site in late January 2014. This is when it was first learned that there was more to Diagon Alley than just the one name. Potterphiles had heard of Knockturn Alley, but what about Horizant Alley or Carkitt Market? They aren't just inventions of Universal Creative, but named by Rowling herself.

The entrance to Diagon Alley was termed "some sort of representation of a moving wall feature" through which visitors accessed Diagon Alley. Not much could be seen of Knockturn Alley, which was "cloaked in darkness as it was completely covered." In Diagon Alley, however, the media guests saw Weasleys' Wizard Wheezes, the Leaky Cauldron, Madam Malkins Magic Menagerie, and Florean Fortescue's. At the end of the block was Gringotts Wizard Bank, but it wasn't open to the tour. The media were told "that the column where the fire-breathing dragon will sit is eventually going to be about twice as high as it currently is." There were a number of other shops, but most appeared to be façades and there was still considerable construction underway on other shops of varying sizes. One thing of note was that there was "no sense of technology anywhere in Diagon Alley. Guests will get the feeling that everything is either manual, gas-powered, machines, mechanical devices, or magic."

In late May, the dragon entered the park. Wingless and lifted by a huge crane, it was placed amidst extensive scaffolding on top of Gringotts. Later the wings arrived and were lifted into place by a crane. The sculptor of the massive dragon was Bryn Court, a north London artist who specializes in TV, film, and commission work. In addition to the dragon, he sculpted many other statues around the park and worked on all of the Harry Potter films. He is currently senior art director for Universal Creative.

Around the same time, sharp-eyed visitors had seen the Hogwarts Express chugging and puffing along its tracks, hauling a coal car and three passenger cars on its test runs to Hogsmeade and back.

Three weeks before opening, Universal held a press conference in the Leaky Cauldron with a panel consisting of Mark Woodbury (president of Universal Creative), Alan Gilmore (art director for the Harry Potter films), Thierry Coup (senior vice president of Universal Creative), and Dale Mason, (director of creative development for Universal Creative). The four spoke about what was involved in creating Universal's second Harry Potter land, as well as the differences and influences of the filmmaking process on the project.

"Gringotts was a ride waiting to happen, and the chance to bring that to life was an opportunity we just didn't want to miss," Mark Woodbury said. There was a continuity problem, however, as Universal Creative wanted a scene in the attraction involving Bellatrix Lestrange and Voldemort that was not in the books or films. "It was a tricky piece of business to find a way to do that that would be authentic, so we studied it pretty hard, and we figured out that there was a slice in time by which we would be enabled to be in the Gringotts Bank in the moment when Harry, Ron, and Hermione were breaking in to steal the horcrux and we found an opportunity to place ourselves in that action. It took a lot of thought; it took a lot of consideration to find a way to allow us to be in that moment in the movie." Rowling studied their idea and decided that it could have happened.

Wizarding World of Harry Potter—Diagon Alley opened on Tuesday, July 8, 2014. Thousands of people began gathering outside the park before the sun came up. The lineup was not as long as it had been for the 2010 opening of Hogsmeade, but it did extend around the lagoon and through the park. The first visitors were not allowed in until 8:00 a.m.

The opening ceremony was not widely publicized and had only been announced three weeks ahead of the event whereas the 2010 opening had had many months of advance notice. There had already been several soft openings a few days previous designed to cut down on the hordes who would attend on opening day. These soft openings, also known as technical rehearsals, could happen at any time and fans have been known to hang around outside attractions under construction for hours, or for many consecutive days, in the hopes of getting an advance ride on a new attraction. Employees in the know were told to deny that any soft openings were about to happen until the last possible moment.

The Diagon Alley opening was to be a low-key affair that included a red carpet and the usual fireworks and rain of confetti before Potterphiles rushed into the park. For some it was an emotional experience ranging from smiles to tears. There was a "receiving line" of wizard and witch team members on the red carpet as the first visitors came in. Not surprisingly, some visitors had to wait for up to six hours for the Escape from Gringotts dark ride that morning. Most riders proclaimed it was worth the wait. Even though three trains were running, the Hogwarts Express attraction caused visitors a further two-hour wait if they wanted to go to Hogsmeade.

Unlike Hogsmeade, which has three attractions, Diagon Alley has only two, if you count the Hogwarts Express which is between the two parks and part of both. To do the attractions in chronological order, as Harry Potter came across them in the books and films, we'll start in the newest section, the City of London.

A great deal of discussion between Rowling, Warner Bros., and Universal Creative about the entrance to Diagon Alley led to the decision to place it fronting Universal Studios Lagoon. More elbow room was also a priority in the new park and the shops and pedestrian walkways were to be larger to accommodate more guests. Maximum capacity would be twice that of Hogsmeade, at 8,000 visitors.

The London façade was constructed to shield Diagon Alley from the rest of the park and from prying Muggle eyes. This area is called London Waterfront, even though the real King's Cross is nowhere near any body of water. Constructed in a semi-circle, the façade stretches from the San Francisco area on the left to World Expo on the right, and is an attraction of its own. Here there are photo ops, food stands, exclusive merchandise, and live entertainment often leading to guests lingering longer than they had expected to do. Only the abundant sunshine and having so many London landmarks within proximity of each other would make guests think they were not in London.

The purple, three-decker Knight Bus is parked next to a replica of the Eros Fountain from London's Piccadilly Circus on a small roundabout in front. The conductor remains in character if guests wish to chat him up and the shrunken head dangling over the dashboard can be quite chatty in its Caribbean accent as it interacts with the conductor and guests. Guests are not permitted inside the bus but, they can look in at the highly detailed props from *Harry Potter and the Prisoner of Azkaban*, including the chandelier and beds provided for weary witches and wizards on their way to London.

(The fountain statue actually portrays Anteros, Eros' twin brother. Eros, known to ancient Greeks as Cupid, is the god of erotic love, while Anteros is the god of selfless love. The statue was built in 1886 as a memorial to Anthony Ashley-Cooper, 7th Earl of Shaftesbury.)

Between the Universal Studios lagoon and the row of some of the largest and most detailed façades in Universal Studios is a beautiful park, filled with trees and benches for the weary visitor, and surrounded by ornate lamp posts and black wrought-iron fences.

A re-creation of King's Cross Station is to the left of the London façade and here guests will embark and disembark from the Hogwarts Express. Next to the station is Charing Cross Road (where a Gringotts Bank ATM can be found), an entrance to the Leaky Cauldron, Secred & Sons ("2nd and 3rd hand books"), Record Shop ("old, rare and new"), Leicester Square Station (the underground) where the entrance to Diagon Alley is located, Wyndham's Theatre (the exit from the Wizarding World), and Grimmauld Place. Number 12 Grimmauld Place is the ancestral home of the Black family and the Black's house-elf, Kreacher, can be seen every few minutes, peeking through the curtains of a window on the second floor.

The London façade is as close to the real-world buildings as possible, except that the area is seriously compacted. The illusion is such that if visitors did not consult their maps or did not already know how to access Diagon Alley, it is not apparent that anything other than London is represented here.

There is also an iconic red telephone booth in front of the record store where, if one dials 62442 (MAGIC), they will be connected to the Ministry of Magic. On either end of the façade are Cabman's Shelters. These were an innovation of the aforementioned philanthropic Earl of Shaftsbury designed to permit hackney carriage (taxi) drivers a chance to grab a bite to eat while on duty. They were the first drive-through food stops in London. One of these sells traditional London food (jacket potatoes and crisps), the other sells exclusive merchandise. Street buskers are sometimes stationed in the area greeting guests and playing a variety of instruments.

The entrance to Diagon Alley in the books and films is through a courtyard in the rear of a popular wizarding pub in London known as the Leaky Cauldron. The pub appears to Muggles to be a broken-down shop on Charing Cross Road between a bookstore and a record shop. The Leaky Cauldron was built in the early 1500s by the first landlady, Daisy Dodderidge, and boasted a bar, dining room, several parlour rooms, and bedrooms on the upper floors. After looking around at the sights upon first entering Diagon Alley, guests should look behind themselves, as above the entrance they will see the small room where Harry Potter lived when he stayed in the Leaky Cauldron in *Harry Potter and the Prisoner of Azkaban*.

The entrance to the Wizarding World's Diagon Alley is next to the Leicester Square marquee and is unmarked. Universal attendants will obtrusively point the way to any Muggles who seem uncertain. The entrance is through a brick wall that does not actually move, but is unseen from outside. The wall reportedly contains 7,456 bricks and weighs over 18.5 tons.

A street map of Wizarding World's Diagon Alley would show Knockturn Alley to the left just past the Leaky Cauldron as visitors enter, Carkitt Market is to the right, and Diagon Alley down the center. At the end of Diagon Alley visitors can see Horizont Alley and Gringotts Bank.

Knockturn Alley is a walkthrough attraction. The covered area is in perpetual night with a projected sky above the faux shop windows filled with spooky special effects. There is a single shop that can be entered and dark arts merchandise purchased. This is Borgin and Burkes (established in 1863), purveyor of "a wide variety of Dark objects such as Death Eater masks, skulls and other sinister objects." On display is the Hand of Glory from *Harry Potter and the Chamber of Secrets* and the Vanishing Cabinet from *Harry Potter and the Half-Blood Prince*, complete with a chirping bird inside. Eric Baker and his team took six months to reproduce the 12-foot cabinet. The props on the second floor are straight from the films and the giant hand in the window was reproduced from molds found in the Warner Bros. studios in Leavesden.

Borgin and Burkes, at 13B, specialize in "objects with unusual and powerful properties" that are "both unusual and ancient." The shop is operated by Mr. Borgin and Caractacus Burke, two wizards who buy cheap and sell high. Harry Potter first visits the shop by accident in *Harry Potter and the Chamber of Secrets* after traveling by floo powder and ending up in a large, dimly lit, dusty shop. Tom Riddle (later Lord Voldemort) once worked in the shop after he graduated from Hogwarts and began collecting the items he would later use as horcruxes.

The other shops are façades with fascinating windows displays for guests to view. Cobb & Webbs is a dark arts shop, run by a witch and mentioned only in *Harry Potter and the Chamber of Secrets* video game. Noggin & Bonce specializes in shrunken heads and has a window facing the alley with shrunken heads floating in a liquid. Using an interactive wand will make the heads sing. This shop is unique to Wizarding World's Knockturn Alley. Dystyl Phaelanges is another shop unique to this park. It is the first display window seen upon entering Knockturn Alley and has an exhibit of skeletons in the front window. The shop specializes in bones, fangs, fossils, and whatever can be made from them. A skeleton in the window will do whatever you are doing if you use your interactive wand on it. The skulls on display are those of a giant, house-elf and pixie created by Eric Baker's team over the course of three weeks with a 3D printer.

Carkitt Market, on the opposite side, is the entertainment district. In this covered area, live shows are staged every half hour or so. With the opening of Diagon Alley, the shows put on by Celestina Warbeck and the Banshees and the stage show by the Wizarding Academy of Dramatic Arts were both moved from Hogsmeade to a stage in Carkitt Market. Here, as before, Celestina sings the classic wizarding hits "You Charmed the Heart Right Out of Me," "You Stole My Cauldron But You Can't Have My Heart," and "A Cauldron Full of Hot, Strong Love."

The retelling of two of Beedle the Bard's classic tales was also moved from Hogsmeade. The wizarding favorites "The Fountain of Fair Fortune" and "The Tale of Three Brothers" are performed using puppetry and scenic props.

There are two refreshment areas in Carkitt Market. Eternelle's Elixir of Refreshment is a food cart selling a variety of beverages, some mentioned in the books and films, such as Draught of Peace, Babbling Beverage, and Elixir to Induce Euphoria, and another, the Fire Protection Potion, which can only be found in a Playstation video game. The drinks are made by combining the aforementioned potions with gillywater for a "delightful flavour surprise."

Next is a wizarding pub known as the Hopping Pot. The walk-up counter derived its name from the Beedle the Bard tale, "The Wizard and the Hopping Pot" and is unique to Wizarding World. They serve the well-known drinks Butterbeer, Pumpkin Juice, and Gillywater as well as a few unique to Wizarding World: Dragon Scale, Fishy Green Ale, Otter's Fizzy Orange Juice, Peachtree Fizzing Tea, Tongue Tying Lemon Squash, Wizard's Brew, and the popular Muggle drink, draught beer.

Most of the shops in Carkitt Market are façades, or simply references made with signs on the walls. There is the blacksmith shop next to the Hopping Pot, probably named for Bowman E. Wright, the inventor of the Golden Snitch, displaying objects of steel and wrought iron. It is unique to the park. The interactive wand will assemble the armor parts in the window into a complete knight and cause a bellows to move up and down. There is a set of troll armor hanging in an alcove nearby that took a blacksmith eight months to forge. In order to make it look authentic and battle scarred, Eric Baker and art director Alan Gilmore battered it with a sword.

Cogg and Bell Clockmakers make and repair all wizarding time pieces, and Concordia and Plunkett Musical Instruments specialize in cellos, bagpipes, lutes, and harps.

Dr. Filibuster's Fireworks is a relatively new establishment that originally sold its products through Gambol and Japes Wizarding Joke Shop. The Weasley twins and Lee Jordan bought the Fabulous Wet-Start, No-Heat Fireworks there in *Harry Potter and the Chamber of Secrets*. With their own unique shop in Carkitt Market, they now sell their pyrotechnics without the middle man.

The Fambus Station Wagon is a photo op featuring an extra-long broomstick, available in five different colors, capable of seating an entire family of six that was produced by the Nimbus Racing Broom Company.

Even wizards need help planning their vacations and in Diagon Alley their needs are met at Globus Mundi Travel Agents in a second-story office.

For those elves without someone to provide service for, there is a House-Elf Placement Agency to provide house-elf allocation services, found only in the park. Chimney Sweep Elf was a service offered in which one could rent a house-elf for chimney sweep purposes. The interactive wand will cause an elf to climb up a chimney on the floor above.

Jellied Eel Shop is a pie and mash shop unique to Wizarding World that has a window filled with stewed and jellied eels and advertises haddock and eels and mash.

The Mermaid Fountain in Hogsmeade has a twin here in Diagon Alley in the square where Diagon Alley and Carkitt Market intersect. The mermaid is like the ones seen in *Harry Potter and the Goblet of Fire*. The interactive wand will turn on the water fountain and, if the mermaid gets tired of turning on the water, she will spit water at the spell caster.

The Museum of Muggle Curiosities has a number of curious Muggle items on display. Located between Dr. Filibuster's Fireworks and Cogg and Bell Clockmakers, only in this park, it exhibits desk lamps, radios, electric fans, televisions, electronics, and microwave ovens.

There is an Owl Post Office here as well as in Hogsmeade, but it is not open to the public so is probably just a way station for owls on long trips or a sorting depot of sorts.

At Shutterbuttons guests can create a moving portrait of themselves. There are 12 scenes inside the shop, each from a site in Hogsmeade or Diagon Alley, where guests can do a bit of acting and leave with a DVD photo album in a collectible tin. Shutterbutton's Photography Studio shares a building with Concordia and Plunkett Musical Instruments and the traveling wizard can fill his luggage requirements and other magical bag needs at Stowe & Packers Magical Bags.

Sugarplums Sweet Shop is unique to this Diagon Alley and has a wealth of wizard treats, from Bertie Bott's Every-Flavour Beans to Exploding Bonbons, Cauldron Cakes, and Acid Pops.

If someone is in a hurry for their wand and doesn't want to go through the elaborate ceremony at Ollivanders, then Wands by Gregorovitch is the place for them. This is probably a British branch of Mykew Gregorovitch's original shop in Europe known as Gregorovitch Zauberstäbe. Like Ollivanders, this shop sells wands of various woods, but Gregorovitch's wands often tend to be plainer and less ornate than Ollivander's. Gregorovitch was once the possessor of the Elder Wand until it was stolen from him. He was killed by Lord Voldemort when the Dark Lord was searching for the wand.

The well turned-out wizard would likely get his haircuts, shaves, mustache sculpting, beard trimming, and scalp treatments at Weeoanwhisker's Barber Shop in Horizont Alley, next-door to Cogg and Bell Clockmakers, only in this park.

Now that the outlying alleys have been explored, let's have a look at Diagon Alley itself.

One of the many façades on Diagon Alley is Broomstix, a shop with an obvious product.

The Daily Prophet has an office here, again a façade. The present editor is Barnabas Cuffe who works out of the Diagon Alley office. This wizarding newspaper is the primary source of news for British wizards, but unfortunately it lacks in journalistic integrity, being more concerned with selling papers than factual reporting. *The Daily Prophet* has a morning and evening editions, but as news changes, an edition can magically change as well.

Mr. Mulpepper's Apothecary is one of two chemist shops in Diagon Alley. Both are façades. Cleaning Solutions and Restorative Draughts can be purchased here by wizards. The other shop is Slug & Jiggers Apothecary, established in 1207, selling potions and potion ingredients. There is a set of shark teeth in the window paying tribute to the attraction that was once here, and the interactive wand, if pointed at a bucket of dragon dung, will cause a foul smell to be emitted.

Eeylops Owl Emporium is one of a chain of shops that sells owls and supplies necessary to care for them. This is a façade, but Hagrid bought Harry Potter's owl, Hedwig, as a birthday present in an Eeylops store.

Florean Fortescue's Ice Cream Parlour was owned and operated by Florean Fortescue before he disappeared when his shop was raided by Death Eaters and subsequently boarded up. In the books the parlour is a small shop with places to sit down inside and a small area outside with a bunch of tables and chairs. Inside, there is lots of colorful ice cream on display. In 1993, Harry spent a lot of time at the parlour doing his homework while Mr. Fortescue helped him and gave him free ice cream every half-hour in *Harry Potter and the Prisoner of Azkaban*. In the park it is a quick-service shop serving two dozen exclusive flavors of ice cream including chocolate chili, clotted cream, and sticky toffee. It also serves tarts, scones, cookies, beverages, and other goodies.

Flourish and Blotts Bookseller is where most Hogwarts students purchase their schoolbooks. The shop has had a few problems with certain books, such as *The Invisible Book of Invisibility* which was never found but cost them a great deal of money, and *The Monster Book of Monsters* which tore each other up and bit the manager when he tried to get one out. This version is a façade.

The Fountain of Fair Fortune is unique to this park, selling Butterbeer, Gillywater, Fishy Ale, Dragon Scale, and Wizard's Brew. It is named after one of the *Tales of Beedle the Bard* and according to Rowling is her favorite of the Bard's tales which could account for its appearance in the park.

The Leaky Cauldron is a popular wizarding pub and inn and is the entrance to Diagon Alley through the rear of the pub. The popular establishment was built by Daisy Dodderidge in the early 1500s. In the books and films, it had a bar, several private parlour rooms, and a large dining room. Muggles saw it as a broken-down old shop on Charing Cross Road. In the park guests will find themselves under a cathedral-like ceiling and feast upon such British fare as Fisherman's Pie, Bangers and Mash, Toad in the Hole, and Ploughman's Platter. There are supposedly two entrances in the park, one from inside Diagon Alley, the other from the London Waterfront side. The latter, however, is a non-opening replica of the pub door as seen in the film. Hungry guests order their meals at the counter and are seated at a table with a candlestick that directs servers where to deliver the food.

Madam Malkin's Robes for All Occasions is where Hogwarts students buy their Hogwarts school uniforms. They have a selection of dress robes and on occasion an invisibility cloak. Guests can buy authentic replicas of Dumbledore's robes or Hermione's Yule Ball gown.

Don't be shocked if the mirror in the shop offers an insulting and unsolicited critique of your outfit. There is also a selection of Hogwarts uniforms, scarfs, ties, sweaters, and jewelry.

The original Ollivanders wand shop (founded in 382 BC) is located in Diagon Alley. It has long been acknowledged that the Ollivander family are the best wandmakers in Britain. Most magic folk purchased their wands here, including Harry Potter. When the Wizarding World Diagon Alley opened, the counterpart of Ollivanders in Hogsmeade became a branch store run by an associate of Garrick Ollivander. The Diagon Alley version is larger with a "towering wall revealing thousands of boxes stacked to the ceiling" and has three rooms off the main store for the wand show to take place. Guests may take part in the wand-chooses-the-wizard show or simply buy any wand they choose. Wand sets, character wands, and interactive wands are all available here. The interactive wands come with a map of Hogsmeade and Diagon Alley and are usable in both parks. Once a wand has been purchased, visitors then consult their maps and seek out the metallic plaques on the ground in front of various objects or shop fronts. By standing on the plaque, waving the wand as directed, and reciting the spell (the last is not necessary but adds to the experience), the magic will activate a different outcome at each site. In the event of problems with the interactive wands, and apparently this is not unusual as the heads have a tendency to fall off, there is a Wand Repair (founded in 1796) specializing in the repair of damaged wands.

Potage's Cauldron Shop is one of the first shops encountered when entering Diagon Alley. Another façade shop, it advertises and displays all types of cauldrons. In *Harry Potter and the Philosopher's Stone*, Madame Potage displayed some in a stack outside the shop, under a sign which read: "Cauldrons—All Sizes—Copper, Brass, Pewter Silver—Self-Stirring—Collapsible."

Before the Wizarding World Diagon Alley opening, Potage's Cauldron Shop façade was located in Hogsmeade. It was replaced by Ceridwen's Cauldrons after the expansion.

Quality Quidditch Supplies has "everything you need to play the most popular sport in the wizarding world." This is where Harry Potter saw his first broomstick, the Nimbus 2000, and later the Nimbus 2001 and the Firebolt. Here guests can purchase Quidditch sweaters, golden snitches, bludger bats, bludgers, brooms, quaffles, and many other items related to Quidditch.

There is a moving poster for the Chudley Cannons on one of the walls. The broomstick designs were created by Pierre Bohanna, head props designer for the Harry Potter movies. There is an old-fashioned Quidditch uniform in a case inside the shop based on one seen in the moving portraits found in the Gryffindor Common Room in Universal's Hogwarts castle.

Even the restrooms have magic. Under the name Public Conveniences is an umbrella and if one has an interactive wand handy they can say the words, make the gesture, and have water pour down from the umbrella. A mischievous wizard might wait for an unsuspecting Muggle to pass underneath. Inside, guests will hear Moaning Myrtle complaining.

Spindlewards, a sewing shop, is a bit of an enigma. This façade shop is not mentioned in any of the films, books, or games from Harry Potter canon.

Weasleys' Wizard Wheezes, also known as Weasley & Weasley, is a joke shop founded by Fred and George Weasley. They began their entrepreneurial enterprise as an "owl-post service" selling joke products from their home at the Burrow. Having little interest in a formal education, their performance at Hogwarts was not ideal. Their patience was tried to the breaking point during the tenure of Professor Umbridge in *Harry Potter and the Order of the Phoenix*. The twins left school and set up, with the help of the donation of his Triwizard Tournament prize from Harry, their own shop. The store is easily recognized by its huge marquee featuring a colourfully striped suited figure tipping his top hat to reveal a rabbit on his head, then no rabbit, then a rabbit, etc. The shop contains not only practical joke items but also defensive magical objects and Fred and George's own line of WonderWitch products including love potions and Ten-Second Pimple Vanishers. When a guest adopts one of the ever-popular Pygmy Puffs, a bell will ring and the pet's name is announced to the shop. For those wizards interested in the Muggle world, there is a small section of Muggle Magic Tricks as well.

Visitors to the Weasley's shop in Wizarding World will want to look up at the ceiling to see the "never-ending fireworks" explosions as they shop for magical toys, tricks, and jokes including "U-No-Poo pills, Skiving Snackboxes, and Puking Pastilles" as well as "Sneakoscopes, Bombtastic Bombs, Peruvian Instant Darkness Powder, Decoy Detonators, Extendable Ears," and more. Listen closely and you will hear whispers coming from the Extendable Ears hanging from the ceiling. There are two floors in this shop, but only the lower is open to Muggles. Using the interactive wand on the toilet in the window will cause a U-No-Poo sign to swirl about.

The last roadway to explore is Horizont Alley, named specifically for the park by Rowling as a play on 'horizontal' as complementary to 'diagonal' for the other alley. Here visitors will find Scribbulus Writing Implements. Though not mentioned by name in the books, it was shown in the *Harry Potter and the Chamber of Secrets* special features DVD. This shop specializes in writing implements, quills, and parchment and ink, and had a counterpart in Hogsmeade. In Wizarding

World guests can purchase any of the aforementioned as well as backpacks, notebooks, bookmarks, journals, envelopes, postcards, and stationery sets. Flicking an interactive wand at the blank parchment in the window will cause words to appear related to wand lore, and in another window a feather to float, re-creating the levitation scene from *Harry Potter and the Philosopher's Stone*.

Flimflam's Lanterns, located in Horizon Alley by an archway leading to Knockturn Alley, specializes in lighting devices. The lanterns here can be turned on and off through the use of the interactive wand.

In addition to the main bank, there is a Gringotts Money Exchange located just down the street. Here Muggles can exchange their currency for wizard dollars in $10 and $20 denominations to either spend or keep as souvenirs. The Money Exchange also has a few souvenirs, like wallets, for your newly acquired wizard bills, chocolate coin candy, and Gringotts Bank bags. The goblin attendant responds to questions.

Wiseacre's Wizarding Equipment sells a wide variety of magical instruments. This is another of those establishments not mentioned in the books, but referred to in the *Harry Potter and the Chamber of Secrets* DVD and confirmed on Pottermore. Before the Wizarding World Diagon Alley expansion, Wiseacre's Wizarding Equipment was a façade in Hogsmeade that was renamed Madam Puddifoot's Tea Shop. The new Wiseacre's is an actual shop with a variety of wizard wares and supplies "including crystal balls, telescopes, binoculars, armillary spheres, compasses, magnifying glasses, moon charts, globes of the moon, crystal phials and hourglasses" along with unique accessories and apparel from Hogwarts houses. On display is the microscope seen with Bill Weasley in the Escape From Gringotts pre-ride show and a barometer that appeared in the films in Dumbledore's office (*Harry Potter and the Half-Blood Prince*) and the Room of Requirement (*Harry Potter and the Deathly Hallows*). An interactive wand causes the stars on a projected star map to be activated.

There is a very crowded pet store in Diagon Alley where Hermione Granger purchased her pet Kneazle, Crookshanks. Magical Menagerie in Wizarding World does not sell live pets, but a close version thereof in the form of plush toys or stuffies. There is every magical beast, from Cornish pixies and Pygmy Puffs to assorted owls, including Hedwig, as well as Crookshanks, Scabbers, Buckbeak, Fluffy, Fang, and Luna's favorite, the Crumple Horned Snorkack. *From Fantastic Beasts and Where to Find Them* there are also Demiguises and Graphorns. The snake in the front window will speak to you in Parseltongue and English, reminiscent of the scene in *Harry Potter and the Philosopher's Stone*. The phoenix in the window will speak if encouraged by an interactive wand.

Another façade storefront on Horizont Alley, Pilliwinkle's Playthings, sells toys that would appeal more to young wizards and witches than Muggles. In the front display window is a scene inspired by a troll tapestry in Hogwarts showing dancing troll marionettes in ballet tutus. The Dancing Feet spell from the interactive wand will compel them to dance about.

The primary and most popular attraction in Diagon Alley is Gringotts Bank. The structure dominates the end of Diagon Alley not only due to its imposing height and architecture but because there is a Ukrainian ironbelly dragon perched on top of it breathing fire every 10 or 15 minutes. To enable visitors to have their cameras ready, the beast gives a growl before belching fire. The temperature of the dragon's fire is said to reach 3,500 degrees Fahrenheit. The dragon is not always operating due to weather restrictions.

Guests enter Gringotts Bank through the front door to find themselves in a cavernous room as seen in *Harry Potter and the Philosopher's Stone* when Harry and Hagrid first entered the establishment, Harry to get some money, Hagrid "on Hogwarts' business." In the first movie, the interior of Australia House in London was used to film the grand entrance hall. When it was time to return to Gringotts for *Harry Potter and the Deathly Hallows—Part 2*, filming would have been impossible on location due to the appearance of a dragon, so a set based on but not an exact replica of Australia House was constructed at Leavesden Studio. Differences included windows in the studio set, the pattern of the marble floor, and the design of the huge chandeliers.

The Leavesden set is replicated in the park, complete with goblin tellers. As guests pass by they can be seen quietly doing banking business by counting money and making notes in their ledgers with quill pens. Periodically they may glance up to acknowledge the presence of Muggles, but do not speak to them. Initially, guests were able to mingle with the goblins under the watchful eye of security guards, but stanchions were later put in place to keep the Muggles at a respectful distance. They are close enough to admire the incredible detail, but not close enough to touch.

At the far end of the faux marble-columned lobby, the head teller will sometimes deign to speak to guests and point them in the direction they need to go to enter the Gringotts vaults. Once in the back corridors, staff members will offer "security ID photos" taken with typically retro wizarding cameras which can be purchased as a souvenir at the end of the ride.

Once in the queue guests will see many items from the films on display such as moving and unmoving portraits of goblin luminaries, copies of *The Daily Prophet* with moving photos, office doors with familiar goblin names on the windows, and the lower-priced vaults on the upper levels. Other items of interest include the moving picture of the Weasleys in Egypt, seen in *Harry Potter and the Prisoner of Azkaban*, and a Gringotts Bank cart that is under repair. This cart was built using specifications for the actual cart that Harry, Ron, and Hermione rode on their way down into the vaults. Made of steel, resin, and fiberglass it weighs around 3,500 pounds.

Further along the queue familiar silhouettes are seen behind one of the office doors as Harry, Ron, and Hermione are conspiring to enter the bank. Apparently, guests have arrived at the very moment in *Harry Potter and the Deathly Hallows* that the trio are about to attempt the recovery of the horcrux from Bellatrix Lastrange's vault.

Bill Weasley's office affords guests with a look at the latest in ultra-high-speed film technology as Bill and the goblin Blordak converse with each other and the visitors. Props and set pieces add depth and credibility to the scene. Blordak is a goblin unique to this attraction. In the queue he has an office opposite Ragnok's (a bank employee, activist for goblin rights, and author of *Little People, Big Plans*) and is charged with showing new clients to their vaults.

The elevators only appear to move as they drop nine miles underground to the Gringotts vaults. As a final warning, guests are shown one of the 12 passenger cars twisting and turning and bumping its way into the vaults while a goblin portrait reads out the usual warnings to pregnant and health problem guests. "You must be at least 42 inches in height to ride, unless you are a goblin." The illusion of movement is provided by projections on the walls moving upwards.

Once the doors open again, guests are instructed to pick up 3D safety goggles, climb a flight of stairs, and clamber into the two-car, twelve-passenger coaster trains that dispatch guests every 80 seconds. Bill Weasley and his goblin buddy Blordak appear again and offer to guide guests to the vaults. The abrupt appearance of Bellatrix thwarts those plans as she casts a nasty blue lightning bolt spell at the guests and sends their cart careening out of control. Speeding through the dark, the car drops and turns and finally comes to a stop before a second screen where Bill and Blordak speak to guests just as Harry and the gang arrive on another cart. Harry tells Bill, "Get them out of here, there's going to be trouble." Having said that the two carts are knocked off their tracks by trolls in suits of armor. In an effort to escape, the guest cars plunge through darkness again only to wind up confronting the gigantic trolls once more. Trolls, guests, and carts plunge into a seemingly bottomless crevasse until the guest car is saved by a spell cast by Bill Weasley. No sooner has Bill told guests how Gringotts is "perfectly safe" than the dragon appears and breathes fire at him. Bill puts the fire out with a water spell and Harry and friends chase the dragon away. The car continues on until Blordak appears and directs them in a different direction which leads r into a bursting wall and the jaws of the snake Nagini, accompanied by the Dark Lord and Bellatrix. Voldemort wants to know where Harry Potter is and Bellatrix emphasizes the question with her nasty blue lightning spell sending the car speeding away again. Voldemort and Bellatrix follow and confront the guests again. Voldemort casts a fire bolt spell, but the dragon, carrying Harry, Ron, and Hermione, appears and attacks the bad guys who vanish. Harry calls to the guest to follow him and the dragon, leading to another plunge through darkness. The dragon appears again, Ron tells Bill, "We got what we came for, take care of them," and the dragon-riding trio begin climbing out of Gringotts. Bill reminds guests that Gringotts is "the safest place of Earth."Cue "Hedwig's Theme" and a gentle ride to the unloading station.

Escape From Gringotts' innovative vehicle capabilities enable it to come to a complete stop before rotating independently to face the required screen. At times the carts move sideways and later rotate back into place as the ride progresses. This feature can make the ride disorienting and the 4K high-definition 3D imagery envelopes visitors in a state-of-the-art attraction. Unlike Harry Potter and the Forbidden Journey in Hogsmeade, which is more of a "Best of Harry Potter' tour," Escape From Gringotts focuses on a single incident from the stories for a more "story-driven experience." True, this story did not actually happen in the books, but Rowling signed off on the concept when it was first presented to her by Universal Creative three years previous. She decided that "the storyline proposed for this attraction was plausible" and "just because these scenes weren't recounted in the books and/or depicted onscreen, doesn't mean that they also couldn't have happened." In fact, according to Mark Woodbury, president of Universal Creative, Rowling wrote the lines Bill Weasley speaks at the end of the ride.

Placing a small train station in Hogsmeade as a terminus for the Hogwarts Express was a simple affair, as the village was already protected by concealment spells to shield it from Muggles eyes. Placing a second station in the heart of Muggle London, however, was sure to challenge "even the Muggles' notorious determination not to notice magic when it was exploding in front of their faces."

Evangeline Orpington, minister of magic from 1849 to 1855, came up with the solution of constructing a concealed platform for wizards and witches in the newly built King's Cross Station that opened in 1852. Except for an occasional mishap that was quickly covered up by Memory Charm from a Ministry of Magic employee on hand, the arrangement worked well.

With the beginning of construction in Diagon Alley it was necessary to provide continuity in getting guests from Hogsmeade in Islands of Adventure to Diagon Alley in Universal Studios, a separate park. According to Thierry Coup, "That created the whole idea of the Hogwarts Express. Of course, we had a parked Hogwarts Express, now taking the journey is another way to give our guests...anyone and everyone can ride the train...there's no limitation, no ride-height limitation."

The obvious solution was to have the Hogwarts Express run from Hogsmeade Station to King's Cross Station and back again. This also necessitated the purchasing of park-to-park admission tickets for those who wanted to ride, a feat easily accomplished at the gate.

Guests will want to ride the train both ways as the experience is different. London to Hogsmeade is beset by peril as Dementors board the train, while the trip from Hogsmeade to London is light-hearted.

When the stations were constructed, the one at Hogsmeade had limited space to expand into and so is much smaller than the expansive area relegated to King's Cross Station. If there is a long line, and it can sometimes jump from a short wait to over an hour for no apparent reason, there is a small snack stand in King's Cross for those feeling a bit peckish.

Hogsmeade Station is based on the set used in the Harry Potter films. When the expansion was completed, the train that had been sitting just inside the entrance was removed and an entrance path to Hogsmeade Station installed.

As construction continued, sharp-eyed guests noticed that by the end of August 2013, six passenger cars and two tenders had arrived in the backstage area awaiting assembly. The first of the two replica locomotives, manufactured by the Doppelmayr Garaventa Group, was installed in position by huge cranes on October 23, 2013. It was placed on a 5-foot, 10-7/8 inch broad-gauge funicular elevated track that runs the 2,218 feet between stations. There is a two-track passing loop halfway so that two trains can run at the same time. By early December a second locomotive had arrived and been tested. The trains do not run on their own steam but are moved with a pull rope, counter-rope system operated from a cable winding motor at King's Cross. The trains run simultaneously, traveling 7.6 miles per hour, each carrying a maximum load of 336 passengers at a time in three passenger cars. The Hogwarts Express enters Hogsmade Station forwards and King's Cross backwards so that the trains are only seen from one side, allowing less detail needed on the unseen side.

When a survey suggested that guests would consider the Hogwarts Express to be an attraction as well as a transportation system, the original plan for only two cars was increased to three. The locomotives are based on the steam train used in the films, a GWR 4900 Class 5972 Olton Hall (as 5972 Hogwarts Castle), and were constructed from aluminum and glass-reinforced plastics with an artificial weathering process applied to give the appearance of an historic train.

The video and sound components and the computer system that control the trains was installed by Frey AG. The video components of the curved window screen which acts as the exterior view window was designed by Double Negative. The music played throughout the trip was recorded at Abbey Road Studio by the London Symphony Orchestra in March 2014 and is called "Connector Train—Hogsmeade to London."

Throughout the first months of 2014, Universal Orlando released concept animation and other bits of information to keep expectations high. On June 24, the announcement came that Diagon Alley and the Hogwarts Express would open on July 8 after almost two-and-a-half years in development. A week before that date, the Hogwarts Express had an unannounced soft opening on July 1, 2014, a week before the rest of Diagon Alley was revealed. One million guests traveled on the train within the first month.

King's Cross Station Universal is a quarter-scale replica of the King's Cross Station in London and is the entrance to the Hogwarts Express ride. Upon entering the station building, guests have their tickets checked and upgraded if they don't have a two-park pass. They then enter the queue and make their way into the building which is well equipped for queue lines. There is a departures sign but there is no mention of Hogsmeade Station as we are still in the Muggle world and if asked team members have no idea what you are talking about if you mention Platform 9¾. The posters are typical travel or advertising posters—"Visit London" on one and "Make a Little Magic" on another. (Professor Dumbledore stands in front of a poster similar to the latter in *Harry Potter and the Deathly Hallows—Part 2*.) As they wind through the queue lines, guests pass by piles of luggage on a platform, suitcases in all sizes, shapes, and colors. After climbing a staircase they arrive at Platforms 9 and 10, and looking through a mirror ahead can see the queue in front of them disappearing through a wall as if by…magic. Actually, it is a special-effects technique known as Pepper's Ghost created by reflecting an image off of plexiglass. It was popularized by John Henry Pepper in a magic show in 1862. It can only be seen by people farther back in the line; once visitors go through the portal themselves they hear only a whooshing sound.

After a few more turns guests arrive at the fabled Platform 9¾, pass a pile of luggage that includes an animatronic white owl, and await the arrival of the next train. The Hogwarts Express pulls in, steam belching and backing into position, as riders from Hogsmeade disembark and the new crowd gets on board the three passenger cars. The attention to detail inside the train is astonishing and accurate.

The compartment doors close as the train starts moving; this also serves to screen whatever is going on in the hallway. Out the large window London can be seen as well as an owl flying by with a package clutched in its talons. In the corridor, silhouettes appear on the windows of the door and Harry, Ron, and someone who is supposed to be Hermione, but doesn't sound like her, are talking about looking for a vacant compartment and something to eat just as the Trolley Witch happens by.

Looking out the window again it is getting dark and stormy and Malfoy Manor is in the distance. Something is materializing in the darkness, a voice cries out "Dementors!" and a shadow appears on the compartment doors just as Harry arrives and uses his Patronus charm to drive the foul things away. The silhouettes of Harry, Ron, Hermione, and the Trolley Witch return, but as Ron attempts to purchase some chocolate frogs they escape and have to be rounded up by the Trolley Witch.

Meanwhile, outside the window Rubeus Hagrid is flying alongside the train on his motorcycle toward the welcoming lights from Hogwarts Castle in the distance. Hagrid turns on the after-burners and takes off in a blaze of fire followed shortly by a flying blue Ford Anglia which careens about beside the train. The car lands in a forest area, skids, and finally crashes into a bridge support. Hogwarts can now be seen closer up across the Black Lake as Hogsmeade Station approaches. Hagrid waves as the train enters the station. Compartment doors open and visitors file out of the train, through Hogsmeade Station, and down a path to the village itself.

The return trip from Hogsmeade to King's Cross begins in much the same way as the previous journey, though the inside queues are not as long. Tickets are checked at the entrance where the static Hogwarts Express display once stood. Most of the queue is outside on the winding flagstone path leading to the station through a forest. During the walk, visitors are serenaded with theme songs from the films. The interior of the station is larger than it appears from outside and require guests to climb a few stairs to get to the loading platform.

As the train leaves the platform, Hagrid can be seen out the window waving goodbye, and Harry, Ron, and Hermione are at the door, once again looking for an unoccupied compartment. Out the window Hogwarts can be seen in the distance, in daylight this time, and Buckbeak the hippogriff flies along side the train for a time. Passing by the Forbidden Forest a number of centaurs can be seen running by, but they stop when they get to the edge of the forest and are replaced by Fred and George Weasley. The twins are swooping by on their brooms waving to the train and carousing with each other until one tosses some fireworks into the sky that explodes and spells out "Weasley's Wizard Wheezes now at Diagon Alley."

The sky turns threatening again as the train enters a tunnel and passes Malfoy Manor. Harry, Hermione, and Ron pass in the corridor, still looking for a compartment and something to eat. A spider appears on the glass that Harry grabs and eats, explaining it is a licorice spider. Ron is not amused.

The train enters the suburbs of London where the Knight Bus is seen in the distance and then closer up as it squeezes between two buildings, swerves through traffic, and shrinks to go under a bridge. As King's Cross Station comes in sight, passengers are greeted with a wave from "Mad-Eye" Moody.

Once the train has stopped, guests disembark at King's Cross Station and make their way through the station and back out into the London Waterfront area. In its first year of operation the Hogwarts Express carried over five million passengers.

During the Christmas season, Universal Orlando decks their themed halls to celebrate new experiences. The Wizarding World offers holiday-themed entertainment in both Hogsmeade and Diagon Alley. Each evening, a projection-mapping show wraps Hogwarts Castle in "holiday inspired imagery" of a special-effects-laden extravaganza with lighting effects, lasers, pyrotechnics, and synchronized soundtracks.

To prepare space for viewing the spectacle, a number of trees were removed from in front of Hogwarts both to provide a better view without branches in the way and to accommodate more guests.

In addition to the show at night, the streets and shops of Hogsmeade and Diagon Alley are "aglow with Christmas lights and décor" and even the Hogwarts Express gets into the holiday spirit. The menus of the eating establishments in both parks feature seasonal treats like hot Butterbeer.

Towards the end of July 2017, Universal announced on their official blog that they were permanently closing Dragon Challenge, with the last day of operation being September 4. In typical Universal style, they did not release specifics of what would replace the attraction, but they did give some clues. "This all-new thrill ride will take you deeper into J.K. Rowling's Wizarding World, where you will encounter some of your favorite characters and creatures. It'll be unlike anything we've ever done before and it will be fun for the entire family," Kristen Clark wrote. "The new attraction will be one of the most highly themed coaster experiences we've created. It will combine a new level of storytelling with an action-packed adventure...and a few surprises along the way."

The park is once again collaborating with both Warner Bros. and the production design team from the Harry Potter films to bring the new coaster experience to life. Clark ended by saying that it's going to "redefine the category and transport you to thrilling places, drawing you into even more exciting adventures within the wizarding world. It's going to be the perfect addition to Hogsmeade." The statement was confirmed when it was noted that a new series of permits that referenced "Project 942" had been issued to Universal on July 28, shortly after their announcement. The permits include demolition of the existing structure and the construction of office trailers that will probably house the teams building the new project.

Riders were evacuated from Hogwarts Express on August 17, 2017, when a technical issue caused the train to stop between stations at about 3:15 p.m. Resort spokesperson Alyson Lundell said that the attraction was cleared of passengers by about 4 p.m. No one was injured, but some riders required assistance for heat issues, though no one was hospitalized. One passenger complained about the lack of quick emergency response. A helicopter flew over the train, which could be seen stopped on the track with a fire truck and an ambulance nearby. Public relations vice president Tom Schroder said at 4:30 p.m. that all guests were safely off the train, but he did not disclose a reason for the evacuation. The ride was closed shortly afterwards for evaluation.

CHAPTER SEVEN
WARNER BROS. STUDIO TOURS LEAVESDEN

Every film that takes place in J. K. Rowling's Wizarding Worlds, from *Harry Potter and the Philosopher's Stone* to *Fantastic Beasts and Where to Find Them* was shot primarily at Warner Bros. Studios, Leavesden. It was the logical choice being the only film studio in Great Britain capable of housing large-scale film productions, and the Harry Potter series certainly fell within that category.

Leavesden began life in 1940 as a British airfield constructed by the De Havilland Aircraft Company and the British Air Ministry at the beginning of World War II. Situated in Hertfordshire about 20 miles northwest of London between Watford and Abbots Langley, the airfield was named for the nearby village of Leavesden. The site, an empty plot of land belonging to the Watford Corporation, was requisitioned by the Ministry of Supply. In time, de Havilland built hangers and runways suitable for use by large aircraft as well as factories to produce Mosquito bombers. To cover the enormous expense of the construction, part of the land was leased to London Aircraft Production and the Second Aircraft Group. These groups produced the Handley Page Halifax heavy bomber.

During the war, large numbers of skilled and unskilled laborers, over half of whom were female, were drafted to work in the factory. The aircraft they produced were critical to Britain's survival in the conflict. By war's end, Leavesden was, by volume, one of the largest aircraft factories in the world. The runways were used to test and later deliver the planes constructed in the factories, and along with the control tower, remain on site today. The former has become the main road into the complex and the latter is an observation lounge.

De Havilland purchased the property after the war and it subsequently changed hands over the years. Hawker Siddeley took over in 1959 and Rolls Royce later began manufacturing aircraft and helicopter engines. As Britain's manufacturing industry declined in the 1980s, Rolls Royce sold their interests in the site and the land lay unused and virtually abandoned.

In 1994, Eon Productions was looking for a place to film their latest James Bond movie, *GoldenEye*. Their usual go-to location was booked, as Pinewood Studios had not expected a rebirth of the Bond franchise. A search revealed the existence of Leavesden, whose tall, open hangers were perfectly suited for converting into sound stages. The land was leased and work began on converting the aircraft factory into a working film studio with the appropriate offices, workshops, and stages. The site was nicknamed "Cubbywood," after Eon's producer Albert R. "Cubby" Broccoli, though the official name was now Leavesden Studios. With the completion of *GoldenEye*, other productions were soon underway including George Lucas' *Star Wars I: The Phantom Menace* and Tim Burton's *Sleepy Hollow*.

Meanwhile, David Heyman had opened a production office in London that he called Heyday Films. Heyman's goal was to make books into films, and with that in mind he began contacting agents and publishers. One of his employees, Tanya Seghatchian, had contacted an agent whose name she had found in a trade publication and requested a copy of a soon-to-be-published book by an unknown author. The story was about a young wizard and when the manuscript arrived Tanya put in on a shelf with other manuscripts to be read. Their procedure was to take books home on Fridays, read and critique them over the weekend, and report their findings on Monday. One day in early 1997, Nisha Parti, secretary for Heyday Films, took a book off the low-priority shelf to read over the weekend. On the following Monday morning, as the manuscripts from the weekend were discussed, Parti told them about this manuscript she had read and loved. It was called *Harry Potter and the Philosopher's Stone*. Heyman was skeptical about the title, but when Parti told him what it was about his interest was piqued and he took it home to read. He had only planned to read a few pages, but by 3:00 a.m. he was still reading and did not stop until he was finished.

The story resonated with him; the boarding school, the students, and the teachers all brought back strong memories of his own days in school. He thought it "might make a good, modestly sized, British film." Heyman had previously made a deal with Warner Bros. to give them first crack at anything his company found that would make a good film. To that end he contacted an old friend and expatriate, Lionel Wigram, in Los Angeles. Wigram presented the book at Warner's weekly development meeting. The response was lukewarm, but he did get a go-ahead to start negotiations, with the proviso, "Don't spend too much money."

It was early 1998 before the deal was closed and Heyman and Wigram began looking for a screen writer. By this time *Harry Potter and the Philosopher's Stone* was doing reasonably well in Britain but was still unknown in the United States, so their quest for a screenwriter was fruitless. When Scholastic bought the rights and published *Harry Potter and the Sorcerer's Stone*, Heyman recalled that almost overnight "suddenly everyone was calling."

Writer Steve Kloves met with J.K. Rowling in Los Angeles with Heyman and Warner executives Polly Cohen, Lionel Wigram, and Lorenzo di Bonaventura. In the studio commissary over lunch, Heyman commented that Rowling "realized she'd found a kindred spirit."

Kloves was hired to write the screenplay and would go on to write seven of the eight movies. *Harry Potter and the Order of the Phoenix* was written by Michael Goldenberg when Kloves wanted a break.

The next decision to make was whether to animate the film and whether they should make a movie combining the first two books or film one book at a time. Rowling had already announced it would be a seven-book series but at this stage everyone was still very cautious about this new commodity.

Heyman was as enthusiastic as he was when he first read the book. Chris Columbus was hired to direct and Stuart Craig, a three-time Academy Award winner, was to be the films' production designer. It had been decided in meetings with Heyman, Rowling, and her agent, Christopher Little, that the filmmakers would keep the cast British and would stay as true to the books as possible. A strong working relationship developed between Rowling, Columbus, Kloves, and Heyman as they fine-tuned the script. Columbus believed that "it was incredibly important to be as faithful as possible, making a film of each book and bringing to life their world as it was written."

With the major staff in place and auditions underway for the actors to play the key roles, the next step was to find a place to film the series. It had long ago been decided to keep production in Britain, but neither of the famous studios, Shepperton or Pinewood, met their requirements. The films would require large spaces and areas that could be tailored to the needs of the filmmakers.

Roy Button, vice president of Warner Bros. Feature Production UK, took Heyman to see Leavesden Studio in Hertfordshire. Here was eighty acres of land and half-a-million square feet of production space, ample for what Heyman required. The site was acquired by Heyday Films on behalf of Warner Bros. for the filming of the first of the Harry Potter films, *Harry Potter and the Philosopher's Stone*. Over the following ten years all the Harry Potter series would be based out of Leavesden.

As the rest of the books were still being written while the first books were filmed, Warner Bros. chose to store all the props and sets on site in the event they might be required again in a future film. As many of the buildings used to store the sets had not been upgraded in many years, some of them tended to leak and lacked soundproofing, so a program to improve the facilities was begun. During the time that the Harry Potter films were being made, the studio was used by other productions as well. *Sweeney Todd: The Demon Barber of Fleet Street* and *Sherlock Holmes: A Game of Shadows*, being set in Victorian times, found it convenient to use some of the standing Harry Potter sets while filming.

Stuart Craig, the production designer, had first read the Harry Potter books on a plane flying to an interview with Chris Columbus and David Heyman in Los Angeles. So, when the men met, Craig already had many ideas about how sets would look; "the books were absolutely stuffed full of potential," he said.

Since building an entire wizarding world was beyond the scope of their budget for the first film, a search for locations was begun. A visual representation of Hogwarts School was a priority for Craig, and he wanted it to look a thousand years old and to appear real. He felt the best way to do that was to join the familiar with the fantastic. He used Gloucester Cathedral, Oxford's Christ Church College, and Durham Cathedral as inspirations.

Set decorator Stephenie McMillan, an old friend and collaborator of Craig's, was brought in to dress and decorate his sets. She was responsible for bringing to life everything from the Dursley's knickknack-strewn parlor and Snape's potions class to stocking full-sized shops in Diagon Alley. Some props, like the students' desks, did double duty and were moved from class to class; other props were unique to each scene.

Another important addition to the staff in the early days of production was Judianna Makovsky, a costume designer. Her first task was to design the Hogwarts student uniforms which had not been mentioned in the books. She based them on the traditional Eton uniforms, but added cloaks, house colored scarfs, and pointed hats. Harry's costumes early in the films would be oversized hand-me-downs from his cousin, Dudley Dursley.

As these preparations were being made, auditions continued. Robbie Coltrane was one of the first hired when he was cast as Rubeus Hagrid followed by Richard Harris as Headmaster Albus Dumbledore and Alan Rickman as potions professor Severus Snape. Ian Hart was chosen to portray Professor Quirrell, Dame Maggie Smith became Professor Minerva McGonagall, and Miriam Margolyes was to be herbology teacher Professor Pomona Sprout. The major student parts were cast last. Tom Felton auditioned for the parts of both Harry and Ron, but was cast as Draco Malfoy. Emma Watson secured the role of Hermione Granger early on, Rupert Grint became Ron Weasley, Matthew Lewis was to be Neville Longbottom, and Bonnie Wright had a small part as Ginny Weasley. It was not until June 2000, two months before principal photography was slated to begin, that Daniel Radcliffe was cast to play the titular role of Harry Potter.

Daniel, Emma, and Rupert were called in to David Heyman's office at Leavesden Studio. Daniel already knew he had the part, but Emma and Rupert were to learn it that day. Photography sessions and press conferences followed as the journey to Hogwarts began.

The first scene to be filmed was the last in the movie. On September 29, 2000, Daniel, Rupert, Emma, and Robbie Coltrane, along with about 150 extras, assembled in North Yorkshire at Goathland's railway station. Later location shots would be done at Alwick Castle, Northumberland, which served as the outside of Hogwarts, the backdrop for Madame Hooch's flying lesson.

Having the cast and crew away from Leavesden and on location gave Craig and Stephenie McMillan the opportunity to put the finishing touches on the sets they were building for Diagon Alley. Craig described his concept of Diagon Alley as "very narrow and very tall...everything is about the window and the stall board outside. ... We played with impossible angles, making that part of the sculptural design, the way the buildings lean and defy gravity." McMillan referred to the construction of Diagon Alley as one of her proudest achievements particularly after Rowling toured the set and pronounced it "as exactly as she had imagined it from the book."

Gringotts Bank was another problem and building it was not within the budget for the film. Craig opted instead to go on location to Australia House in London. The London Zoo became the site of Harry's first brush with a snake speaking parseltongue and assorted staircases and rooms in various London buildings, schools, and cathedrals stood in for interior shots of Hogwarts. The site for Platform 9¾ did not fit well between Platforms 9 and 10 at King's Cross Station, so Platforms 4 and 5 were substituted. The appearance of the Hogwarts Express at King's Cross caused curious crowds to form as filming progressed.

The largest studio set built by Craig at this time was the Great Hall. Eventually, it would be the site of the Sorting Ceremony, wizard chess games, the Dueling Club, feasts, and general get-togethers of friends. Originally, several hundred candles were hung by wires from the ceiling until the wire on one overheated and snapped. "We did not think it wise to risk the lives of four hundred children sitting in the Great Hall. So, we lost the candles," Heyman remarked later. Digital candles were substituted.

When Rowling toured the set for the first time, the Great Hall set was the first one she saw. Months before she had shown the designers a sketch of how she envisioned the hall to look. Now, she felt like she was walking into that drawing, "It's a real room—it's not all plaster and spit holding everything together," she was quoted as saying in *Harry, A History*.

The Great Hall was built to last. Despite the fact that an artificial floor would have been less expensive and more versatile, Craig insisted on genuine York stone slabs. His decision turned out to be sound as the Great Hall survived ten years of filming. Besides the Great Hall set, only two other sets remained unchanged throughout the eight films: the Gryffinder Common Room and Professor Dumbledore's office. According to Craig "They got a fresh coat of paint a couple of times. But there they were, there forever."

A 1:24-scale model of Hogwarts castle was built on one of the soundstages at Shepperton Studios in Surrey under Craig's direction and with a special models unit from Cinesite. It took 86 artists and crew members to construct the first version which was then rebuilt and altered many times for the next seven films. As the original outdoors location shots were made at Alnwick Castle and Durham Cathedral, details from those structures were incorporated into the model. The doors were hinged to open, the windows were glazed, tiny owls perched in the owlery, the Astronomy Tower had tiny telescopes and astrolabes, and the model was wired to light up for night shots.

Exterior filming of Privet Drive where Harry lived with the Dursley family, "the worst sort of Muggles imaginable," was done on location at Bracknell, west of London. The less-than-tasteful interior sets, parlor, kitchen, and cupboard under the stairs were constructed at Leavesden. Only *Harry Potter and the Philosopher's Stone* was filmed on location as the bright lights at night, the commotion of action during the day, and the owls caused some trepidation amongst the locals. For the rest of the series, Number 4 Privet Drive and vicinity was re-created at Leavesden.

Some of the cast and crew had begun filming *Harry Potter and the Chamber of Secrets* before the premiere of *Harry Potter and the Philosopher's Stone*, a sign of how confident Warner Bros. was in the success of the franchise. New sets had to be built, primarily the Chamber of Secrets, but also the book store, Flourish and Blotts, where Gilderoy Lockhart was first introduced; the herbology greenhouse where the students learned about mandrakes; the Whomping Willow where the newly crafted Ford Anglia crashed; and Ollivanders where Harry purchased his first wand. Also new to the second film was the Weasley's home at the Burrow and the dark and an expanded Forbidden Forest.

Many changes were made with *Harry Potter and the Prisoner of Azkaban*. Not only did Chris Columbus step down as director, replaced by Alfonso Cuarón, but the death of Richard Harris required the casting Michael Gambon as the new Albus Dumbledore. Cuarón would change the tone of the films, make them somewhat darker, and also have a redesign done to Hagrid's Hut and the grounds of Hogwarts.

Amongst the new sets would be the Shrieking Shack where Peter Pettigrew was unmasked, the bridge out of Hogwarts where Remus Lupin and Harry talked about his parents, Professor Trelawney's Divination classroom, a partial Three Broomsticks interior, and the fabled Knight Bus that carried Harry from Privet Drive to the Leaky Cauldron.

Hogsmeade would make its first appearance in *Harry Potter and the Prisoner of Azkaban* and the full-sized sets constructed for the film were reproduced in miniature. Again, the attention to detail was incredible, with tiny merchandise in miniature window displays, cauldrons piled up outside of Potage's Cauldron Shop, brooms for Spintwiches, and quills for Scrivenshafts. Everything had to be hand-made, for easily found dollhouse items seldom included owl cages or cauldrons. When it was finished the model of Hogsmeade, second only to that of Hogwarts in size, had to be dusted with "snow" (actually dentric salt) that was sprinkled from a cherry picker overhead.

Harry Potter and the Goblet of Fire was to be directed by Mike Newell, the series' first British director. As the longest of Rowling's books to date, it would prove more difficult to pare down to movie size without losing a lot of the story. Making *Harry Potter and the Goblet of Fire* into two movies was considered at one time, but as Mike Newell noted: "While there was enough content in the books to make two movies, there wasn't really enough story to make two."

For the Yule Ball, everything in the Great Hall was redecorated in ice and silver, from the beams to the Christmas tree to the window mullions. The Wizengamot scene had to have a new set as did the spectator stands for the Triwizard Tournament and the dragon arena, which was one of the largest sets to be constructed. Stuart Craig noted: "When you are battling a dragon, you need space."

The same was true for the second challenge in the Black Lake which would require the filmmakers to construct the largest water tank in Europe. The tank took six months to build and was 60 by 20 by 20 feet. It had to be kept clear for filming, so it had a filtration system capable of cycling the half-a-million gallons of water every ninety minutes. Construction time was spent teaching Radcliffe to scuba dive and to do so with prosthetic gills as well as hand and feet extensions.

The maze in the third challenge was mainly computer generated imagery (CGI) with the addition of hydraulic twenty-foot high leafy walls that could move and twist in on the actors. The final set, the Angel of Death statue in the graveyard by the church in Little Hangleton, was where Cedric was killed and Harry dueled with Voldemort. It was another of the larger sets and had to be built indoors so that filming could be done during the day and to contain the fog affect, as any little breeze would blow it away.

David Yates, the director of *Harry Potter and the Order of the Phoenix*, was a relative unknown to feature films. His expertise lay in television shows where he had directed award-winning and critically acclaimed programs.

Once again, large sets were needed: the façade for Grimmauld Place, the interior sets for the Order of the Phoenix headquarters, the Hog's Head Inn, and the Room of Requirement. The set for the Ministry of Magic, where Voldemort and Dumbledore battled with fire and water, challenged even state-of-the-art CGI. The sequence ended with the shattering of 250 glass windows which had to be cleaned up and the atrium rebuilt so that the sequence that would take place before the fight could be filmed.

When Professor Horace Slughorn (Jim Broadbent) was recruited by Dumbledore in *Harry Potter and the Half-Blood Prince*, one of his conditions for returning to Hogwarts was a new office larger than "the water closet I had before." Craig and McMillan set to work refurbishing the Room of Requirement set into "something very Victorian and very pompous, as he is." There was a fireplace, a desk, dark brown drapes over large windows, ornate columns overstuffed chairs and Chesterfields, and a grand piano in the corner. This one character also required the interior and exterior of a Muggle house; his old, smaller office for flashback scenes; an interior set of the Three Broomsticks; and a set for his Slug Club parties.

What would have been the largest set created for the films had it been made was the cave in which Voldemort had hidden one of his horcruxes. The entrance to the cave was a location shot of the Cliffs of Moher in Ireland, but the interior was mostly green screen and digital. Only the rock walls just inside and the rocky outcropping on which most of the action takes place were constructed sets.

At first David Heyman was reluctant to divide *Harry Potter and the Deathly Hallows* into two films. He soon realized that there was so much that had to be resolved and explained "emotionally and physically that we would have had to leave out, it would have meant that resolution would be unsatisfactory." Yates and screenwriter Steve Kloves agreed, Kloves even going so far as to suggest that perhaps it should be three films. Warner Bros., despite the cynics who suggested it was just "one last dash to the till," told the filmmakers to do "whatever you decide is creatively the right way to go."

So, two films it was, but they would have to be shot simultaneously. A grueling eighteen months of continuous filming lay ahead to guarantee the availability of the entire required cast and crew.

One of the earliest sets was the tent in which Fleur Delacour and Bill Weasley were to be married. As it was assumed that Fleur's parents would pay for the wedding, the French influence, as opposed to the Weasley eccentricity, would be present. McMillan suggested they use a green-and-cream striped tent they had in stock, formerly used at a Buckingham Palace garden party. Craig agreed, but thought more subdued colours like purple and pale grey would be more appropriate. Following that, the interior and the props were also grey and purple, elegant and un-Weasley looking. Black faux-bamboo chairs had a "wizardy" look and black butterflies flitted around the tent poles.

The final battle scene with Hogwarts under siege was accomplished digitally, as to destroy the actual sets would leave bits of Styrofoam and plywood strewn about when there should be stone and rubble. The ruins had to be newly built. To accommodate the battle scenes, many areas, such as staircases, bridges, and courtyards were built larger. A damaged version of the castle model was constructed digitally.

The scenes in the Room of Requirement where Harry searched for Rowena Ravenclaw's diadem and later raced to escape the pursuing fires were created by piling up several thousand pieces of furniture, purchased by McMillan over the preceding months. She also used items from the previous films. "We had thirty-six desks, all the tables from the Great Hall, all the benches, all the professors' stools. The trophy cabinet dressing. The chess pieces from the second film. The party dresses from the Slughorn party," she said. To bulk it all up, plywood boxes were built and the objects piled on only one or two layers on top. CGI helped expand the room and add even more props.

The large, black-tiled Muggle-born Registration Commission room contained forty-eight desks on purple carpets under a vaulted ceiling. Nearby, Dolores Umbridge's office at the Ministry of Magic was toned down to reflect the more somber mood of the final films. The cat plates were present, but the whimsy of having them moving was not repeated. Other items, such as the furniture and pink rugs, were brought over from her office at Hogwarts.

Shell Cottage, where those fleeing from Voldemort found refuge, was prefabricated at Leavesden and moved to Freshwater West beach in Pembrokeshire, Wales, to shoot on location. The structure was reinforced inside with steel scaffolding tubes to prevent wind from blowing it down. Thousands of shells, oyster (for the walls), razor (ridge tiles), and scallop (roof) were used for the exterior and interior sets.

The Godric's Hollow scenes where Harry and Hermione seek out the graves of Harry's parents and encounter Bathilda Bagshot, were shot in Lavenham, Suffolk, and at Pinewood Studios. There was already a huge cedar tree there that Craig wanted the cemetery to be spread out under. That required building the church, graveyard, and village around it and then covering it in an estimated forty tons of snow. The weight destroyed the lawn underneath, but it was carefully restored before the filmmakers departed.

On March 21, 2010, during the filming of *Harry Potter and the Deathly Hallows—Part 2*, a fire broke out on one of the sets. "We were called at 8:27 p.m.," said a spokesperson from the Watford firefighters. "The side of the set had caught fire. The damage to the side that caught fire was fairly extensive." According to magical-menagerie.com, Tony Smith, the watch commander, added: "I think they are filming some stunts for the last scene. There is a big battle scene involving a lot of pyrotechnics and explosions. There is a mocked-up castle made of timber, steel and plastic—somehow it caught alight. By the time we got there the on-site fire crew had it pretty well under control—they did a good job. We just helped damp it down and inspected the area. I didn't see any cast—but there were about 100 crew, who were all evacuated to a marshaling area. They didn't seem too concerned. It's hard to say how much damage was caused, because some of it may have been planned as part of the filming. Perhaps they got much better footage than they expected."

No one was injured and the fire was considered accidental.

The last day of photography on the Harry Potter series was June 12, 2010. It was shot at Leavesden and involved Harry, Ron, and Hermione, and their escape from the ministry with Yaxley in pursuit. Afterward, cast and crew gathered for a barbecue and heartfelt speeches of farewell.

With the completion of the filming of *Harry Potter and the Deathly Hallows*, Warner Bros. purchased Leavesden Studios to use as a permanent European base. By November 2010 the site had been renamed Warner Bros. Studios, Leavesden. Plans were announced to invest over £100 million in redevelopment.

According to a November 8, 2010, press release: "Having received all necessary planning approvals from Three Rivers District Council and Watford Borough Council, Warner Bros. is now set to build on that contribution with the re-development of the 170-acre site that will see the refurbishment and expansion of the studio, increasing its ability to provide for services such as visual effects, prosthetics, animatronics and film editing, as well as expanding the external filming and production areas. This commitment will help to sustain the level of employment generated by the productions based at the studio of approximately 1500 jobs and the creation of around 300 more including building and specialist contractors."

Sound stages A to H would be retrofitted and equipped with the latest in filmmaking technology. All the original structures would remain intact including the runway and control tower. The renovations were expected to be completed and reopened for use for television and film production by 2012.

Part of the redevelopment would include two new sound stages, J and K, designed to house and display "many of the iconic sets, costumes, creatures and props from various Warner Bros. films shot in the UK." This was initially planned as a behind-the-scenes look at the Harry Potter series, which could be seen, with prior booking, by the general public. Several of the film sets would be available to allow guests "the opportunity to witness the exceptional creativity and craftsmanship that went into bringing the film series to life."

This evolved into what would become a permanent public exhibition called the Warner Bros. Studio Tour London—The Making of Harry Potter. The 150,000-square-foot museum would contain some of the most iconic Harry Potter film sets, such as the Gryffindor Common Room and boys' dormitory, the Great Hall, the Ministry of Magic, Dumbledore's office, Snape's potions class, Umbridge's office, the Weasley kitchen, Number 4 Privet Drive, and Harry's cupboard under the stairs.

Boris Johnson, the mayor of London, visited the site before it was completed in December 2011 and remarked that it would become "an important addition to London's tourism itinerary."

Hundreds of people lined the red carpet at the official opening ceremony of the Warner Bros. Studio Tour on March 31, 2012. Many of the actors stopped and chatted with photographers, reporters, and fans; signed autographs; and posed for selfies. Celebrities included producers David Heyman and David Barron; directors David Yates, Mike Newell, and Alfonso Cuaron; and actors Bonnie Wright, Rupert Grint, Tom Felton, Warwick Davis, Evanna Lynch, Nick Moran (Scabior), David Bradley (Argus Filch), Helen McCrory (Narcissa Malfoy), Alfie Enoch (Dean Thomas), Harry Melling (Dudley Dursley), David Thewlis (Remus Lupin), and Natalia Tena (Nymphadora Tonks).

Over a year later, on April 26, 2013, the site was officially opened once again, this time by the Duke and Duchess of Cambridge and Prince Harry. Several hundred beneficiaries of charities they all supported received special invitations to the Studio Tour on the same day as the royals visited. As the visit got underway, the royals were given a talk about the history of the venue right up to modern day to mark the studio's 90th anniversary. They were then shown models, costumes, and props from the latest Batman movie, *The Dark Knight Rises*. The royals later experienced a 3D production set and viewed original sets from some of the Warner Bros. films. After that, they were met by J.K. Rowling, who had been unable to attend the first opening. Prince William then spoke while conducting the royal inauguration of Leavesden. "All three of us have been looking forward to being here with you all today," he said "So far it has exceeded our expectations." The audience laughed when he added, "Harry is just excited to see a real-life talking owl. I haven't yet told him Harry Potter is fictional, so please don't let the secret out just yet."

Prince William went on to praise the Rowling's work: "The journey today began most obviously after the legendary story by inspiring author J.K. Rowling, translating her phenomenal imagination on to paper in the form of the Harry Potter series." Prince William then officially opened the Warner Bros. Studios with a film clapper board.

A meeting of their Charities Forum, a collection of 35 charities of which the royals are patrons, was held in Hogwarts Great Hall. This was followed by the Royals taking the Warner Bros. Studio Tour London—The Making of Harry Potter. They took wand lessons in the Gryffindor Common Room, one of the original movie sets, and engaged in a wand dual.

Touring Diagon Alley they peered in shop windows and were met by Bonnie Wright and Matthew David. At the end of the tour, guides from the studios presented the three with hand-crafted wands and a Harry Potter Tour passport.

Warner Bros. Studio Tour London—The Making of Harry Potter was designed by the Thinkwell Group, a Burbank-based design and production agency in collaboration with Warner Bros. and the film makers, Stuart Craig, Stephenie McMillan, creature designer Nick Dudman, and special-effects supervisor John Richardson.

The name "Studio Tour" was given to the attraction as Warner Bros. had sold a license to Universal to create Harry Potter theme parks and therefore could not use the term "theme park." That is just as well, for strictly speaking it is not a theme park as there are no rides, only displays of theatrical props and sets. The Studio Tour is adjacent to the working film studios where the eight Harry Potter films were made and consists of two sound stages and a backlot containing original sets and vehicles.

The front of J Studio is decorated with huge Harry Potter posters and signage large enough that there is no mistake as to where visitors are to enter the building. High up on the lobby walls are large posters of all the main characters in the films.

The tour can handle about 6,000 visitors a day and the standard, self-guided tour typically takes about three hours. Guided tours are available as are handheld digital guides that contain facts about the costumes, props and sets, and behind-the-scenes footage. A souvenir guidebook ("the ideal piece of memorabilia") is for sale as well. Tickets have allotted entry times and Studio Tours has a Starbucks and Studio Café in the lobby for visitors who arrive early.

Hanging from the ceiling in the lobby is the first prop visitors will see, the flying Ford Anglia. Created for *Harry Potter and the Chamber of Secrets*, the car on display here is the complete, flawless version known to the designers as "Hero." The battered version was referred to as "Rambo.". Throughout the years the Ford Anglia has been moved to different areas of the tour.

In the early days of the beginning of the tour, visitors first encountered the iconic "cupboard under the stairs" from *Harry Potter and the Philosopher's Stone*. It has since been moved to the backlot and installed inside the Number 4 Privet Drive set.

After viewing the film in the Studio Tour Cinema, visitors enter the Great Hall, based on a room in Christ Church College at Oxford. This set was built for *Harry Potter and the Philosopher's Stone* in 2000 and was used in all the films except *Harry Potter and the Deathly Hallows—Part 1*. The main difference between the great hall at Christ Church and that at Hogwarts was the placement of the windows. Those in Christ Church were so high that they would have been out of frame in most shots, so Stuart Craig had them digitally lowered.

This spectacular set is one of the few that guests can walk through. Here they view two large tables along the walls set with plates, goblets, and utensils. The Chocolate Feast created for *Harry Potter and the Goblet of Fire* is displayed on one of the tables. The original desserts were edible, but the ones here are imitation. Along one wall are the flambeaux (torch holders) representing the four Hogwarts houses and the massive stone fireplace. On the other wall are displayed the costumes of many of the teachers. The professor's table is at the end of the room and features the costumes of Professors Moody, Flitwick, Trelawney, McGonagall, Dumbedore, and Snape, as well as Hagrid and Filch. The Owl Podium used by Dumbledore was "covered in real gold and years of melted wax." Behind the table, in the corner, is the seldom seen House Points Counter that is said to have caused a national shortage of Indian glass beads when it was constructed. The ceiling, which in the films shows the sky outside and is festooned with hundreds of candles, is a maze of scaffolding and light fixtures, as that effect was later rendered with CGI.

Scenes for the Yule Ball and the Battle of Hogwarts were filmed here. For the ball, 90 decorators spent an entire month transforming the Great Hall with silvery ice and snow.

A tribute to the directors and producers is next, with boards showing the principals involved in the production of the films and notes about them.

The Set Decoration area contains more of the thousands of costumes that were created for the films. Hundreds of different sizes of school robes had to be made for the extra students as well as the main characters. Daniel Radcliffe's very first set is here. More than 300 costumes were created for the Yule Ball scene alone.

Spooky ghost costumes were made of material that easily could be made transparent with visual effects. Judianna Makovsky was the costume designer who dressed John Clease as Nearly Headless Nick and later admitted she "never laughed so hard in a fitting!" As the resident ghosts come from different eras, Makovsky needed to design costumes that, while historically accurate, "didn't look as if they came out of a period drama."

The Set Decoration exhibit also includes Yule Ball props, including the Taj Mahalish ice sculpture, Professor Slughorn's chocolate feast props, Hogwart's main gate, and hair and make-up examples.

The Gryffindor Common Room and the boys' dormitory were built as two connected sets. On one side there is a doorway that goes nowhere and on the other a staircase that spirals up to a hallway leading to the boys' dormitory set. The paintings in the common room feature Gryffindor's heads of house over the years, including a younger Professor McGonagall. One wall is covered with a tapestry known as *The Lady and the Unicorn*, a fifteenth-century work that the set decorators chose due to the use of Gryffindor colors in the woven material.

The dormitory was the bedroom shared by Harry Potter, Ron Weasley, Dean Thomas, Neville Longbottom, and Seamus Finnigan. The fabric used for the bed curtains was found by Stephenie McMillan in a local shop. As the films progressed and the children aged, the props beside their beds changed to reflect their developing interests. The size of the beds, however, remained the same despite the actors growing in height and in later films they had to lift up their legs to prevent their feet from protruding over the end. Harry's invisibility cloak, used by the visual-effects team, is here. Several varieties of the cloak were made, including one with a bright green inside lining that was replaced by CGI to make Harry appear invisible. Costumiers used a special velvet fabric with ancient runes and Celtic symbols printed onto it. In the common room is a wireless radio with moving lips on the front grill.

The shelves in Dumbledore's office, located in the highest tower of the school, are filled with hundreds of books, many of which are old British phonebooks enhanced with leather and dust. His memories, both his own and from others, which could be viewed in the Memory Cabinet with the Pensieve, are stored in 800 hand-made and labelled vials created by the art department. The headmaster's fascination with the universe is showcased by a working telescope, said to be one of the most expensive props created for the films and seldom seen on screen. The sword of Gryffindor is a real sword with a redesigned hilt. Most of the ornate cabinets on the walls are moveable to allow a variety of camera angles and placements.

The wand display shows numerous wands, each labeled with its owner's name, in a large circle. Pierre Bohanna, the head of the prop department, was responsible for thousands of hand-crafted wands, each one unique to the character who wielded it. Scattered about are suits of armor obviously designed for goblins, the clock from the Astronomy Tower, more costumes, and the Griffin Staircase leading to Professor Dumbledore's office.

Many of the props used throughout the films are on display in glass cases. Props from *Harry Potter and the Goblet of Fire* include the Triwizard Cup, the Goblet of Fire, and the golden dragon egg. From other films are such familiar items as Slughorn's hourglass, the Philosopher's Stone, Neville's Longbottom's Remembrall, a Golden Snitch, the Crystal Goblet from which Dumbledore drank the water covering the horcrux locket from *Harry Potter and the Half-Blood Prince*, a Time Turner, Deluminator, assorted horcrux containers, and Rita Skeeter's Quick-Quotes Quill and notebook.

The potions classroom is one of the larger sets on display. The set was not created until *Harry Potter and the Half-Blood Prince* was filmed and it was much expanded on from the original on-location set in the Sacristy at Lacock Abbey, Wiltshire, with the windows covered to give more of a dungeon appearance. Also shot at this location was Professor Quirrell's Defense Against the Dark Arts class, the Mirror of Erised Room, and the cloister walks of the courtyard.

The graphics department hand made and affixed labels to hundreds of bottles, flasks, and vials to place on shelves around the potions classroom. Some of the bottles contain herbs, dried leaves, and baked animals bones purchased from a local butcher. Bubbling cauldrons; Bunsen burners; large, heavy, wooden desks and stools; and both Professor Snape's and Professor Slughorn's costumes complete the scene. In addition to being the potions classroom, the set also served, with modifications, as Professor Snape's office and initially as the trapdoor room Fluffy was guarding in *Harry Potter and the Philosopher's Stone*.

Professor Lupin's Defense Against the Dark Arts classroom was quite different from the way it had been decorated for the previous teacher, Gilderoy Lockhart. It has the look of a naturalist's taste rather that Lockhart's narcissistic décor. Items from Lupin's travels are scattered about the room as well as the art nouveau-style cabinet to contain the Boggart, an ancient gramophone, and a projection system.

A low, narrow set from the Leaky Cauldron was built for the upstairs hallway outside Harry's room where he stayed the night in *Harry Potter and the Prisoner of Azkaban*. The corridor is in fact only about 10 feet long, but due to forced perspective, it appears to be 50 feet long. In the same area is the massive locking front door seen in *Harry Potter and the Deathly Hallows—Part 2,* a Gringotts cart suspended from the ceiling, Hagrid's motorcycle, a marble moving staircase, and "Mad Eye" Moody's broom and the trunk he had been imprisoned in throughout most of *Harry Potter and the Goblet of Fire*.

The Quidditch display is filled with props related to that favorite Wizard sport. Costumes from several different teams show the evolution of uniforms throughout the films. Each actor had four or five Quidditch costumes and their double had another eight to ten. In the early films the uniforms consisted of a wool sweater, 19th century trousers, hooded robes in house colours, and high boots. For *Harry Potter and the Prisoner of Azkaban*, uniforms were designed for adverse weather conditions. Quidditch brooms range from the Firebolt to the Nimbus 2000 and the Nimbus 2001. Quaffles, bludgers, beater bats, and a myriad of other Quidditch-related items are scattered about.

For those keen to learn how to use a wand, there is an instruction area where visitors get tips on spell casting from an instructor on a video screen as well as a studio guide. Large mirrors on either side of the screen enable the learners to observe their style. There is also a green screen area where visitors can sit with a cake floating over their head or shrink next to giant friends, or have themselves filmed riding on a broom, Later, they can purchase a DVD of the ride complete with a digitally drawn background.

Nearby is the door to Vault 687 from deep underground in the Gringotts vault and the Chamber of Secrets entrance. Both of these portals have intricate mechanisms that shift, click, and turn as the doors are opened, a practical effect created by Mark Bullimore. An electric motor, hidden behind the door, causes the snakes to slither along slotted tracks in the scene from *Harry Potter and the Chamber of Secrets*.

Hagrid's Hut changed in appearance and location for *Harry Potter and the Prisoner of Azkaban* and subsequent films. First seen as a one-room hut filled with the trappings of a groundskeeper, it was built and filmed in Black Park, Buckinghamshire. For the rest of the films in which the hut appeared, it was built at Glencoe in the Scottish Highlands. The original octagonal hut, now in a pumpkin patch, had a second octagon added as a bedroom, necessary for the story but explained as an upgrade for Hagrid who was now the Care of Magical Creatures professor. The ceiling interior of the hut is crowded with ropes and cages containing peculiar creatures. It rained throughout most of the filming and when shooting was done the hut was taken down and re-created at Leavesden with the backgrounds rendered digitally.

The Weasley's kitchen set first appeared in *Harry Potter and the Chamber of Secrets* and contains numerous, seemingly magic-controlled props, some of which are working. All the moving gadgets are mechanically or electronically controlled and created by the special effects department. To reflect Molly Weasley's love of knitting, there is a pair of knitting needles part way through her latest project, in the sink a scrub brush scours a pot, a knife is cutting up a carrot on the counter cutting board, and an old flat iron is taking the creases out of some material on an ironing board.

Few of the items in the house complement each other, as the Weasleys often depended on second-hand mismatched items and other disparate décor. Even the windows and doors seem salvaged from some Muggle renovations and cobbled together. The Weasley clock that indicates the location of each family member was originally a grandfather clock bought at auction. Swinging, spinning parts and pendulums were affixed to the bottom by the prop department and the hands were replaced with scissor blades and photos of the characters attached.

The Burrow was destroyed by fire in *Harry Potter and the Half-Blood Prince* and when Craig and McMillan rebuilt the Weasley home it was less eccentric than before. Furniture was newer, it was less cluttered, the sink and the cast-iron stove had survived the fire, and the white wash was an effort to conceal some salvaged but charred timbers.

The Ministry of Magic sets take up a large area of the sound stage. Amongst them is Umbridge's office as it was in *Harry Potter and the Deathly Hallows—Part 1*. Her ministry office was not as cheerily bright pink as it had been at Hogwarts. More subdued, darker pinks were used to reflect the sober tones of the establishment. The moving kitten plates were gone and only a few non-moving plates were represented. The desk and chairs had been transferred from Hogwarts as well as the carpet.

In the Ministry of Magic atrium stands the black stone "Magic is Might" monument installed after the Death Eaters took over the ministry. It replaced the golden Fountain of Magical Brethren that had been previously located there. The new monument depicts a wizard and witch standing triumphant on a column atop struggling, but fully clothed (they were naked in the book) Muggles in their "rightful" place. The monument contains fifty-eight Muggles, carved from foam and hand painted.

The atrium of the Ministry of Magic is accessible by several means including toilets, telephone boxes, and the fireplace floo powder network. The gilded fireplaces lined both sides of the hallway entrance to the atrium with incoming on one side and outgoing on the other. Nearby were replicas of the Prophecy Orbs from *Harry Potter and the Order of the Phoenix* and crystals from the cave where Voldemort hid his locket horcrux.

While seeking locations and inspiration, Craig and his crew visited the London Underground. The oldest tunnels were constructed in the 1800s and "used an extravagant amount of decorative ceramic tile," Craig noted. As the ministry was underground, it made sense that they would use high-gloss, reflective tiles to provide as much light as possible. The set designers chose to use deep red, green, and black, and huge gilded fireplaces. The tiles, over 30,000 of them, were made from thick cardboard and painted numerous times to give them the look of actual ceramic. The original set, when complete, was over 220 feet long which was quadrupled in size by CGI. The columns of windowed offices overlooking the atrium were 30 feet high as that was as high as the ceiling in the sound stage would permit. That allowed for only two stories; the rest were applied digitally. While filming, hundreds of extras were required, many of whom were crew members with beards, hats, and appropriate costumes.

The next area is a salute to the graphics department where dozens of art directors, concept artists, and illustrators worked to create every prop, character, and design in the Harry Potter films. Every design went through numerous iterations before it was finally deemed perfect. Here, display cases are full of the little details that are often not noticed when the film is being watched, but which add tremendously to its overall feel.

Copies of *The Daily Prophet*, which appeared in every film, are on display. The headlines, in a Gothic font created by Miraphora Mina, and the illegible font used for the actual body of the story, were taken from Victorian newspapers and ads. Those shots that were to include moving pictures on the pages had green screen placed in the appropriate place for later addition. The headline stories were dictated by the scripts, but the rest was left up to the imagination of Mina and Eduardo Lima.

They added horoscopes, crossword puzzles, letters to the editor, smaller news stories, and classifieds, all with an esoteric, wizardly twist. Friends and co-workers often appeared on the pages of *The Daily Prophet*, and even Mina and Lima themselves "were the final contestants in a wizarding duel final."

At least forty editions of *The Daily Prophet* were printed throughout the film series, each with a different front page, though sometimes the interior pages were repeated as no one outside the graphics department saw those. Some editions required only a few copies, others required hundreds. The look of the newspaper changed when the ministry took over, giving it a more dogmatic, totalitarian feel. The headlines sometimes took over the entire front page, such as "Harry Potter Undesirable No 1" and "He Who Must Not Be Named Returns." The ministry editions are distinguished also by the "P" in Prophet being enhanced with gold foil.

The Quibbler, touted as "The Wizarding World's Alternative Voice," was edited, printed, and distributed by Xenophilius Lovegood. The newspaper first appeared in *Harry Potter and the Order of the Phoenix* and had more of a tabloid look than *The Daily Prophet*. As with its competitor, *The Quibbler* used unintelligible fonts for the text and a variety of fonts for headlines. Over 25,000 pages of *The Quibbler* were printed containing articles such as "Secrets of the Ancient Runes," "Goblins Cooked in Pies," "Wrackspurts: Unfuss the Mystery." A special edition for *Harry Potter and the Half-Blood Prince* produced an article of Spectrespecs with a pair of the glasses perforated for removal on the cover.

Other graphics on display include ministry paraphernalia, educational decrees, wanted posters, packaging for Weasley's Wizard Wheezes, school textbooks, *The Life and Lies of Albus Dumbledore*, and *The Tales of Beedle the Bard*.

Visitors now leave the studio and step outside into the backlot where a number of large sets are on display. Hagrid's motorcycle and sidecar, one of seven versions of a 1960 Royal Enfield, remodelled for Hagrid's oversized backside, is here in pristine condition and ready for photo ops should guests wish to sit on it. The Ford Anglia is also parked here for the same purpose.

The other vehicle, the Knight Bus, cannot be entered, but stands here in all its purple, triple-decker glory. The bus was constructed from actual London double-decker buses. The roof was cut off a Routemaster, a deck was added, and the roof replaced. The entire 22-foot-tall bus was then painted purple. A second bus with a more powerful engine was mounted on a turntable for stunt work. An interior set contained beds, a chandelier, and a talking shrunken head. The latter was not mentioned in the books, but Rowling reportedly remarked, "I wish I'd thought of that." Some London streets were closed off for eight nights over an eight-week period to allow filming of the Knight Bus.

The 78-year-old British steam train No. 5972, "Olton Hall," was used as the Hogwarts Express throughout the series. Scenes featuring the train were filmed on a sound stage at Leavesden and on a track running the length of the original 100-acre backlot. For the tour, the train exhibit opened in March 2015 and stands on a set of tracks, puffing steam as visitors mount the platform. Prop luggage with character initials and a luggage trolley disappearing into the brick wall on Platform 9¾ serve as photo ops. The adjoining carriage can be entered and visitors can sit in the set used for filming and watch as the windows demonstrate how some of the scenes, including the Dementor attack and the escape of the chocolate frog, were filmed.

The bridge connecting Hogwarts to Hagrid's Hut was never mentioned in the books; it was an invention of the director, Alfonso Cuarón, for *Harry Potter and the Prisoner of Azkaban*. Only one section of the bridge was built on location in Scotland, but the weather was so rainy that it was moved to Leavesden and the scenes filmed there. The rest of the bridge was computer-generated. This is one of the few props that visitors are permitted to walk around on.

There are two large building façades in the backlot. One is the Tudor-style house constructed to represent the Potter home in Godric's Hollow after it had been damaged during Voldemort's attack on the family. The other is one of the most famous addresses in literature, ranking along with Sherlock Holmes' 22B Baker Street: Number 4 Privet Drive.

The suburban Dursley home where Harry Potter spent the first years of his life, most of it in a cupboard under the stairs, was the only part of the set that was not entirely a façade. Number 4 also included part of the ground floor. When the tour opened, only the façade was available for photo ops. It was later opened to the public in June 2016 after Fiona Shaw (Petunia Dursley) made a tour of the set for the 15th anniversary of *Harry Potter and the Philosopher's Stone*. Guests are now able to walk down the small hallway, past potted plants and hideous wallpaper, see Dudley's certificates, see Harry's tiny cupboard under the stairs, and look into the quirky front room where hundreds of Hogwarts letter are hung on thin wires from the ceiling.

Other props here include the Riddle Family Gravestone; the Angel of Death, inspired by a more benign statue in Highgate Cemetery in North London, and chess pieces from the full-size chess game played by Harry, Ron, and Hermione in *Harry Potter and the Philosopher's Stone*.

The Railway Shop on the platform sells Harry Potter merchandise and a booth nearby sells snacks and Butterbeer should visitors want a break before continuing the tour.

The creature effects department is showcased in the next part of the tour saluting the team of artists, engineers, and sculptors who, using animatronics, make-up, and detailed models, turned concept art into three-dimensional creatures. Hours were required to make the over 60 different goblin masks needed for the final film as well as some 250 body casts for simulating death, petrification, or stunning spells.

Stuart Craig's favorite prop was the *Monster Book of Monsters* that required three versions, one to move about on a pole that was later removed by CGI, one that could be held by the actors, and one that snapped, bit, and shot out shredded paper. Also included in this area are Inferi; Hagrid's half-brother Gawp's head; the Hog's Head prop; Fenir Greyback's appliances to convert David Legeno into a werewolf; Grindylow from the Black Lake; Death Eater masks; Fawkes, the Headmaster's phoenix; Victor Krum's sharkhead form; spiders; basilisk bones; and Charity Burbage's limp form as it hovered over the banquet table in Malfoy Manor before being fed to Nagini.

Next is Diagon Alley. All the façades seen elsewhere in the world are re-created here as well, except these fronts are the originals made for *Harry Potter and the Philosopher's Stone*. Some of the set pieces on this cobbled street were repurposed as Hogsmeade in *Harry Potter and the Prisoner of Azkaban* and were not required as Diagon Alley until *Harry Potter and the Half-Blood Prince* was filmed.

Ollivanders, where many wizards purchased their first wands, is perhaps the most famous of the shops. The interior set contained 17,000 hand-labeled wand boxes. In the early films the wands were quite plain, but as time progressed they were designed as more ornate. It has been estimated that Daniel Radcliffe wore out between 60 to 70 wands during the ten years of filming.

The 20-foot mannequin in the window of Weasley's Wizarding Wheezes tips its hat, but does not have an appearing/disappearing rabbit as seen in the films and theme park. The costume was made from dyed white felt. The storefront was under construction for three months and contains over 120 individual products inside and on display in the windows.

The display of white card models in the next exhibit would send any miniaturist's heart aflutter. These models were made by the art department before actual set construction began and often contain small personal touches that go unnoticed in the films. The models help the director and production designer look at size and scale and determine camera angles. Some of the intricate white card models on display are Hogsmeade, Whomping Willow, Astronomy Tower. Knockturn Alley, the Burrow, Prefect Bathroom, Hagrid's Hut, Quidditch Tower, and the Beauxbaton Carriage.

The final exhibit, and perhaps the *piece de resistance* of the tour, is the breathtaking 1:24 scale model of Hogwarts School of Witchcraft and Wizardry. This art department-constructed model provides a 360-degree view of the castle. A team of 40 artists and crew members built the first version of the Hogwarts model for *Harry Potter and the Philosopher's Stone*. Throughout production more than 50 sculptors, painters, and other artists maintained the model. By the time filming was done, every courtyard, tower, and turret had been filmed and enhanced with digital effects. Filmmakers inserted a tiny lipstick camera into the model to get a perfect point-of-view when planning shots and camera movement.

Many of the courtyards and towers were replicas of areas of Alnwick Castle and Durham Cathedral where scenes from *Harry Potter and the Philosopher's Stone* were shot. Real gravel was used for boulders and rockwork and landscaping was done with actual plants based on areas in the Scottish Highlands where some of the filming was done. Some 300 fiber-optic lights simulate lanterns and torches and the illusion of some students using the hallways. The lights in the exhibit area are dimmed to simulate night as the lights come on and brighten again for a day-time view. The model includes features such as small model owls sitting in the owlery, and the surrounding trees were made with real wood and dried flowers.

The castle is cleaned every six months by the Magic Camera Company who erect scaffolding around and over it. The model unit supervisor, José Granell, explains: "'We bring in a team of technicians who worked on the model during filming. We prepare all the new ground dressing weeks ahead of schedule before we start working on repainting the landscape and placing new trees and vegetation." From adding texture to the rocks to re-glazing the lake, no detail is left out when the team fine-tunes the model.

The Forbidden Forest exhibit wing, about half way through the tour, was opened on March 31, 2017, with the assistance of Evanna Lynch, Jason Isaac (Lucius Malfoy), and James and Oliver Phelps. Chief special-effects make-up artist Nick Dudman explains: "You're entering the creepy, dangerous place. It'll be colder and spookier and nasty things could happen to you. Nothing will eat you, but there might be a moment when you might perhaps suspect that something might."

One of Rubeus Hagrid's original costumes, lantern in hand, ushers guests through the impressive Hogwarts Gates and deep into the forest. The 19 enormous, 12-foot diameter trees were all hand-made over a period of months from molds taken from actual trees. While the trees are impressive from the front, a look behind will reveal hollow, lightweight structures that are hanging from the ceiling.

Stuart Craig described the Forbidden Forest's evolution throughout the films saying: "As you go deeper into the forest, the more the look changed. What you see here is a version of the Forbidden Forest from deep within."

Amongst the trees stands the hippogriff Buckbeak. This version was made especially for the studio tour with the same attention to detail as the film versions. The creature effects team inserted and glued each individual feather. According to Dudman: "One of the biggest challenges was tracking down the original moulds used for Buckbeak." The hippocriff bows to courteous visitors. "It's wonderful. It's been seven months getting it all ready. It's been like rummaging around an old toy box finding your favorites."

Fungi litter the forest floor and sprout from the tree trunks and spider webs appear the deeper into the forest one goes. Further on, the wind moans and lights flicker as huge spiders appear above. The spiders' spindly legs are eerily life-like and all the more convincing when the spiders suddenly descend. Just ahead Aragog, the aromantula, emerges from its dark, cobweb-strewn lair. The massive spider has a leg span of over 18 feet; its hairy body was hand-fitted from hemp, yak hair, and sisal. For his appearance in *Harry Potter and the Chamber of Secrets*, Aragog required 15 technicians to operate him. Aragog is aquatronic rather than animatronic in that he is activated by a water pump which provides more smooth, life-like movements. According to the studio tour website: "Arachnophobes are welcome in the Forbidden Forest. You can ask one of our Interactors to direct you to a spider-free route during your visit."

Last to be seen is a practical model of Harry's patronus that looks like a big furry dog before CGI does its magic. The patronus lights up when a lever is pulled.

Throughout its history the studio tour has offered special entertainment for limited periods of time. In the summer of 2014, at the Harry Potter Summer Screenings event, 2000 guests were offered the chance to watch Harry Potter films where they were produced. All eight films were screened from July 7 to 26 at the studio Tour cinema. The event was in conjunction with the six-week summer feature Bludgers and Broomsticks.

Some of the events, such as Wand Choreography Interactive and the interior of Number 4 Privet Drive, proved so popular that they remained after their respective events closed.

Other events included Wizarding Wardrobes which presented some of the best never-before-seen costumes from the films, from initial design to finished items, and tips on how to make the material look centuries old or battle-worn.

The Dark Arts event gave visitors an opportunity to try out their wand technique against a Death Eater or walk down a spooky Diagon Alley where the lights are dimmed, the music foreboding, and followers of the Dark Lord patrol the street.

A special Breakfast at Hogwarts reception was held around the model of Hogwarts School dramatically lit to simulate daybreak. On August 21 and 28, 2016, at the same time as Finding the Philosopher's Stone (July 22 to September 5, 2016), the house tables in the Great Hall set were also laid out for breakfast time, and included wizarding cereals like Pixie Puffs and Cheeri Owls. The new feature was a continuation of the 15th anniversary celebration of the film version of *Harry Potter and the Philosopher's Stone.* Props from the first film were in abundance, including Fluffy's drool, a moving Devil's Snare, chess pieces, vats of troll boogers, a pool of unicorn blood, and the Philosopher's Stone.

On December 7 and 8, 2016, the spectacular Dinner in the Great Hall event was held. The Great Hall was transformed for Christmas with the props used for that purpose in the films. Guests were given wands of their choice upon arrival and the first of two courses of Christmas dinner with all the trimmings. After a tour of the studio, guests arrived at Platform 9¾ where dessert was served.

Actors Eddie Redmayne (Newt Scamander) and Dan Fogler (Jacob Kowalski), stars of *Fantastic Beasts and Where to Find Them,* surprised fans with a special appearance at the studio tour on March 16, 2017. The pair emerged form the Great Hall to pose for photos after guests had been presented with free Fantastic Beasts posters and replicas of Newt's wand.

An updated version of Scamanders book, *Fantastic Beasts and Where to Find Them,* containing six new magical creatures and a new foreword, was recently published.

CHAPTER EIGHT
INSIDE THE WIZARDING WORLD—JAPAN

On the other side of the world, four years after the opening of The Wizarding World of Harry Potter—Hogsmeade at Universal Studios Orlando and one week after the opening of Wizarding World Harry Potter—Diagon Alley at Islands of Adventure, a third Wizarding World, the first outside of the United States, opened in Osaka, Japan.

The ancient, exclusive, reclusive Japanese wizarding school of Mahoutokoro is located on the volcanic island of Minami Iwo Jima, about 750 miles from the main island of Honshu. A distinctive feature of the school's robes is that student progress in their magical learning is signified by their robes changing color to designate their status. The robes of top students will turn gold and those of students interested in the dark arts, white. The most sought-after wands are crafted from cherry wood.

Quidditch has gained widespread popularity in Japan. Their top player is Tengu of Toyahashi. The Japanese National Team qualified for the 1994 Quidditch World Cup with the entire team riding Nimbus 2000s. They did not make it to the finals that year, but had better luck at the 2014 World Cup in Argentina. That year the team rode Yajirushis, defeating Poland 350 to 140 when Seeker Norito Sato beat Poland's Wladyslaw Wolfke to the snitch in the 59th minute. Japan next played favorites Nigeria and again emerged victorious with a 270 to 100 score. The semi-finals ended their run for the World Cup when they were defeated by Bulgaria 610 to 460. The spectators were aghast when the team followed their usual practice of setting their brooms on fire after a loss.

Dragons are prevalent in Japan, but the only other magical creature mentioned in *Fantastic Beast and Where to Find Them* is the kappa. This critter is a water-dwelling, webbed-handed, scaly monkey-like creature. The kappa, according to Professor Snape, is also found in Mongolia and tends to grab and kill anyone wading in its pond. Politically, Japan has its own Ministry of Magic.

Universal Studios Japan announced in September 2012 that in two years a Wizarding World of Harry Potter would open at its Osaka location, modeled after the Universal Orlando version with Hogwarts Castle as the centerpiece. Like its American counterparts, Universal Studios Japan would partner with Warner Bros. and Universal Parks and Resorts on the project, having struck a licensing deal with both.

As far back as December 1994, Osaka Universal Planning Inc. was established to research opportunities for the development and eventual construction of a large theme park. In less than two years a master agreement had been concluded with Universal (then known as MCA Inc.) for the planning, construction, and operation of a theme park to be known as Universal Studios Japan. The Japanese theme park was initially owned by private investors including Goldman Sachs & Co., one of the oldest and largest investment banking firms; Asian private-equity firm MBK Partners; and U.S. hedge fund Owl Creek Asset Management who had a 49 percent stake in Universal Studios Japan; Comcast NBCUniversal with a 24 percent stake; the City of Osaka; and other Japanese companies.

Osaka Universal Planning Inc. then changed its name to USJ Co. and moved its head office to Suminoe-ku, Osaka. The final contract for Universal Studios Japan was concluded in March 1998 and construction of the new theme park began at Konohana-ku, Osaka.

Opening day was March 31, 2001, and the park promised to bring "authentic entertainment from the two popular American theme parks to Osaka, along with a host of shows and attractions original to Japan." Much like the philosophy of Tokyo Disneyland, the designers were cognizant that the Japanese people wanted an American version of the park, not a Japanese version. Therefore, Universal Studios Japan consisted of Universal Wonderland, Hollywood, New York, San Francisco, Jurassic Park, and Amity Village.

Universal Studios Japan welcomed over 11 million visitors in the first year, setting a record for theme park attendance. Most of the guests were from Japan, South Korea, and other Asian countries as well as Western tourists. Subsequent years averaged 8 million visitors.

To all appearances the park was doing well, but trouble was brewing underneath. *Japan Times* reported in October 2002 that Akira Sakata was resigning his position as president of Universal Studios Japan "to take responsibility for a series of problems at the park" that caused a significant 29 percent drop in attendance from April to September.

A retired government official formerly working for Osaka City, Sakata had been president of Universal Studios Japan since 1999. He apologized to visitors and shareholders, even though he "stressed to reporters that he did what he could to carry out his duties over the past three years and five months at USJ." He was replaced by former Osaka deputy mayor Shin Sasaki.

Japan Times reported: "The park has been hit by various troubles including the use of foods past expiration date at restaurants, burst sewage pipes, industrial water used as drinking water at many water coolers in the park, the inflow of coolants into tap water at the company cafeteria and colon bacillus and Legionella disease detected at the three artificial ponds within the park. In addition, on July 31, it was reported that too much gunpowder was used for attractions. Osaka city eventually banned USJ from using gunpowder, which has had a further negative effect on business. Visitors are especially worried about non-sterilized water from industrial supplies flowing into water coolers at the park, which was caused by misconnected pipes." The Hollywood Magic fireworks show was at the center of the controversy "because it was caught using more explosives than its license called for."

During the ensuing years, the problems were dealt with and more attractions were added to help boost attendance. Two major draws, Sesame Street 4D Movie Magic and Shrek's 4D Adventure, were introduced in 2003, followed by the Amazing Adventures of Spider-Man a year later. Happy Harmony

Celebration, Peter Pan's Neverland, Land of Oz, and Hollywood Dreams—The Ride opened between 2005 and 2007.

The park had celebrated its first five years in style with parades and closed shows, but underneath all was still not well. Universal Studios Japan posted a group net loss of 4.63 billion yen in the year ending March 2006. The company had issued 25 billion yen worth of preferred shares in 2005 to Goldman Sachs and the Development Bank of Japan to help it restructure. Goldman unit Crane was now Universal Studios Japan's top shareholder with 50.97 percent, according to a filing by USJ. Attendance at Universal Studios Japan remained constant, around the 8 to 8.5 million mark.

On May 10, 2012, Universal Studios Japan, in partnership with Warner Bros. and Universal Parks & Resorts, announced that they would be bringing the Wizarding World of Harry Potter to Japan, marking the global expansion of the themed entertainment experience that started at Universal Orlando Resort. The official announcement was made by Glenn Gumpel, president and CEO: "Universal Studios Japan is committed to being the world's best theme park and by bringing this brilliant story to Japan and creating a fantastic experience is yet another validation of that commitment." With him was the governor of Osaka, Ichiro Matsui; the president of Warner Bros Consumer Products, Brad Globe; and the president of Global Business Development Universal Parks and Resorts, Michael Silver. Special guests included James and Oliver Phelps. More than one hundred excited fans, dressed in Harry Potter attire, screamed with delight when the announcement was made. On Monday, October 29, 2012, Universal Studios Japan greeted its 100 millionth visitor since its opening in 2001.

Though not present, J.K. Rowling commented on the announcement: "I was delighted to experience and enjoy the attention to detail, creativity and superb craft that went into the first Wizarding World in Orlando. I am equally delighted that the same level of expertise and enjoyment will translate to the new park in Japan." No one had any doubt about the success of the addition to the park as Stuart Craig, production designer for the Harry Potter films and overseer of the Wizarding Worlds in Florida, would also supervise the Japanese version.

The announcement further promised: "Just as in Orlando, the Wizarding World of Harry Potter at Universal Studios Japan will faithfully and authentically bring to life the stories created by J. K. Rowling in her books and captured on screen in Warner Bros.' films."

The new Wizarding World was expected to "make a significant impact on tourism" and create "thousands of new jobs and bring economic benefits throughout Japan for decades to come."

In addition: "The themed area itself will be a fully immersive environment for the entire family that brings the stories of Harry Potter to life and is faithful to the visual landscape of the films, including a majestic Hogwarts castle which will serve as the centerpiece of the land."

On February 1, 2013, Japan Railway Yumesaki Line, which provides convenient access to Universal Studios Japan, began operation with a train wrap designed in the motif of the Wizarding World of Harry Potter. "The train wrap will feature illustrations of the themed land's landmark Hogwarts castle and images of the beloved characters, Harry, Hermione, and Ron." Thierry Coup flew to Osaka in January 2014 to spend ten days checking progress and testing Harry Potter and the Forbidden Journey to fine-tune the high-tech ride. Coup commented: "What's great about all of these other Harry Potter-themed things that are going into Osaka and Hollywood is that they're all going to have their own unique elements. Things that you can only see and experience if you go to that specific theme park."

Universal Studios Japan hosted an event on April 18, 2014, to "celebrate the announcement of the Grand Opening of The Wizarding World of Harry Potter" slated for July 15, 2014. On hand to mark the occasion were Japan's prime minister, Shinzo Abe; Caroline Kennedy, ambassador of the United States to Japan; Academy Award-winning art director and production designer for the Harry Potter films, Stuart Craig; actress Evanna Lynch (Luna Lovegood); world-renowned architect Tadao Ando; Universal Studios Japan ambassadors; and the Japanese boy band SMAP.

The evening's celebration began with Glenn Gumpel, president and CEO of Universal Studios Japan, receiving an "owl"-delivered letter from Hogwarts. Letter in hand, he greeted the special guests, all of whom received loud applause. Gumpel presented the letter from Hogwarts to Prime Minister Abe and Ambassador Kennedy, who together, reading from the letter, announced the opening date. At that moment, Hogwarts castle was illuminated with a radiant light show with fireworks, which unveiled its towering scale and lit up the night sky. Abe and Kennedy made a few remarks, and then Evanna Lynch led the audience in casting a Lumus charm on the castle which resulted in more dazzling fireworks.

Anticipation for the upcoming Wizarding World is suspected to have caused an upswing in park attendance. For the first time since its opening in 2001, attendance topped the 10 million mark.

A soft opening was held on June 8 when sixty specially invited young Potterphiles, including child celebrities Seishiro and Chieri Kato, gathered in front of Hogwarts Castle wearing house scarves and t-shirts and clutching mugs of Butterbeer. They all raised their mugs to celebrate the introduction of Butterbeer to Japan. Seishiro Kato remarked: "I am so happy to experience Butterbeer mustache, too."

A section of the interior of Hogwarts castle, at the center of the park, was partially revealed. The youngsters were led into the castle to see the moving portraits in the Portrait Gallery.

After more than two years and a cost of 170 million yen, the park was finally finished.

The grand opening celebration began the night before at sundown, Monday, July 14. Some 1000 invited guests arrived and at 7:15 p.m. walked the red carpet to a stage that had been constructed in Hogsmeade village for the event. Twenty-five minutes later, Tom Felton (Draco Malfoy) and Evanna Lunch stepped forward and cast the Lumos charm to illuminate Hogsmeade village and Hogwarts Castle with a display of fireworks and colored confetti, to thunderous cheers.

"The craft and attention to detail across the Wizarding World of Harry Potter at Universal Studios Japan is incredible and I will take away the memory of Hogwarts castle reflected on the Black Lake in particular. I'm delighted that Harry fans in Japan and around Asia can experience a physical incarnation that is so close to what I imagined when writing the books," said Rowling when she visited the area.

Twelve hours later, at 7:15 a.m., the opening ceremony began. Lynch, Felton, and Gumpel stood at the entrance archway to Hogsmeade. Lynch and Felton led the crowd in a Revelio charm, causing the archway to fill with smoke which slowly lifted to reveal the village beyond. Japanese Muggles swarmed through the archway to explore the new attractions.

The website of Universal Studios Japan announced with certainty that the "45 billion yen project with a 5.6 trillion yen projected economic impact over ten years is sure to meet the expectations of a national level project of its size and attract many guests over the coming years." A huge increase in park attendance was noted over the following months.

Butterbeer has proven very popular in Japan, so much so that Universal Studios Japan (USJ) had kept track of how much was being consumed. At 9:56 on the morning of October 24, 2014, the one millionth Butterbeer was served 102 days after the grand opening. To commemorate the occasion, Potterphiles in house colors along with the Frog Choir and the Triwizard Rally performers gathered around the Butterbeer cart in anticipation of the serving of the one millionth cup of Butterbeer. The lucky recipient, Aichi Pre, of Okazaki City, and her family were presented with Hogwarts robes and scarfs, a guided tour of Universal Studios Japan, and all the Butterbeer they could drink for the rest of the day.

One of the differences between the Universal parks in the U.S. and the one in Japan is the capability and passion of the team members. One writer stated that "comparing the competence and enthusiasm of Japanese theme park service to its American counterpart is like pitting Gryffindor against Hufflepuff—it's just not a fair fight." In Japan, costumed workers go to guests to have pictures taken rather than waiting for guests to come to them. They constantly engage with adults and children. "It's not easy to manage the hordes of people who visit Harry's world every day, but the USJ employees make it look easy, keeping lines orderly and preventing shops from reaching critical mass, always with a smile on their faces."

According to the 2014 Theme Index Global Attraction Attendance Report, Universal Studios Japan was ranked fifth among the top 25 amusement/theme parks worldwide, attracting 11.8 million visitors in 2014, 16.8% more than in the previous year.

Never at a loss for occasions to celebrate, the next ceremony was held was on May 21, 2015, when hundreds of Potterphiles bedecked with Hogwarts scarves gathered in the evening as members of SMAP and USJ's ambassadors stepped onto a stage in front of Hogwarts Castle. The ambassadors introduced Tom Felton and Katie Leung (Cho Chang) along with Glenn Gumpel who announced that Harry Potter and the Forbidden Journey, the attraction showing inside Hogwarts, would in future be upgraded from 3D to 4K3D, the only Harry Potter attraction to have this upgrade. To make this happen, Felton and Leung cast a Patronus charm at the castle, causing an eagle, rabbit (Luna Lovegood), weasel (Arthur Weasley), and stag (Harry and James Potter) Patronus to appear on the castle walls followed by a display of fireworks.

Less than a month later, on July 15, the first anniversary of the grand opening of Wizarding World in Osaka was celebrated at the entrance arch to Hogsmeade. The usual group gathered to mark the occasion, along with the Hogwarts Express conductor and students from Durmstrang Institute and Beauxbatons Academy.

The company announced on September 28, 2015, that Comcast NBCUniversal agreed to purchase 51 percent ownership of Universal Studios Japan from the current shareholders. The acquisition was meant to show the strong commitment of Comcast NBCUniversal to grow and evolve Universal Studios Japan and to accelerate the entire group's global strategy in theme park business. On the same day, Glenn Gumpel step down as CEO when the transaction closed. Jean-Louis Bonnier was named as the new CEO.

"Universal Studios Japan will continue to progress along with its basic policies such as the successful marketing strategy which has boosted the attendance these recent years and look forward to even further growth utilizing a financial strength and a great platform Comcast NBCUniversal will give," Gumpel said.

Comcast NBCUniversal wholly owns Universal Studios Hollywood, which includes Universal CityWalk Hollywood. It also owns Universal Orlando Resort, a world-class destination resort featuring two theme parks (Universal Studios Florida and Universal's Islands of Adventure), four resort hotels, and Universal CityWalk Orlando. Comcast NBCUniversal also has license agreements with Universal Studios Japan in Osaka and Universal Studios Singapore at Resorts World Sentosa. In addition, Comcast NBCUniversal has recently announced plans for a theme park in Beijing and an indoor theme park to be developed as part of the Galactica Park project in Moscow.

Christmas in the Wizarding World was slated to be something special for 2015 with the introduction of a new menu item for the winter season. The magnificent Holiday Feast features whole-roasted chickens as well as chipolatas, traditional British gravy and cranberry sauce, and a variety of vegetables. "An elaborate re-creation of snow on the roofs of buildings, icicles, and other details are sure to make you completely immersed in the winter scenery that was frequently described and seen in the original books and films."

Japanese actresses and models Alice and Suzu Hirose, dressed in Gryffindor robes and each holding a wand, introduced a new attraction at Wizarding World at an opening ceremony. On April 13, 2016, Universal Studios Japan began offering two new magical experiences. Wand Magic and Wand Studies offer guests an opportunity to practice and cast spells at different locations within the Harry Potter area. According to a press release, "Following the announcement, the Hirose sisters joined other special guests and Harry Potter fans in casting several spells to the delight of everyone in attendance. After successfully demonstrating the correct way to cast a "Wingardium Leviosa" spell and making a simple feather float in the air, the Hirose sisters then proceeded to cast a "Locomotor" spell which, to the surprise of the audience, resulted in the impressive levitation of the famed Ford Anglia enchanted car seen in the Harry Potter films."

Wand Magic is the name given to the interactive wands experience imported from the Wizarding World in Orlando. As in the U.S. park, guests search for "magical points" in several locations with the assistance of a map. At least two of the charms are unique to Hogsmeade Osaka. The fire-making charm, Incendio, causes flames to spurt from a distant chimney, and Meteolojinx creates a miniature snowfall. "Wand Assistants at respective locations will give 'personal interaction' to each and every guest." Wand Studies is a show-style attraction wherein "students of the four houses of the Hogwarts School of Witchcraft and Wizardry practice how to cast spells while receiving support from guests."

For about two months at the end of 2016, the Wizarding World would experience Moments of Darkness. The event was held in conjunction with the 15th anniversary of the Universal Surprise Hallowe'en, bringing guests a wizarding world they had never seen before. Guests would come face to face with the Death Eaters, purveyors of dark magic, as they appear wearing black hoods and masks, and peaceful Hogsmeade would experience moments of darkness as night falls.

A new limited-edition food, Hallowe'en Dessert Feast, ranging from mountain-shaped chocolate ganache treats to carrot cake, was available during the fall only and consisted of desserts inspired by *Harry Potter and the Philosopher's Stone*. During the day, Magical Trick or Treat saw Hogsmeade villagers handing out sweets.The Wand Magic was extended to a "mysterious wooden barrel" that has appeared in Hogsmeade Village. With each charm successfully cast, the barrel overflows with candy.

Comcast NBCUniversal announced on February 28, 2017, that it had agreed to purchase 49 percent ownership of Universal Studios Japan from its current partners, including Goldman Sachs; former USJ CEO Glenn Gumpel; Asian private-equity firm MBK Partners; and U.S. hedge fund Owl Creek Asset Management. The purchase price for this transaction was 254.8 billion yen ($2.3 billion), valuing Universal Studios Japan at 840 billion yen ($7.4 billion), including the assumption of Universal Studios Japan net debt. Upon completion of the transaction, Comcast NBCUniversal will own 100 percent of the theme park destination.

"Universal Studios Japan is an amazing and incredibly successful theme park," said Tom Williams, chairman and CEO of Universal Parks & Resorts. "This acquisition will bring an even stronger future for the theme park, its guests and its team members. We are thrilled USJ will fully be part of the Universal family and look forward to continuing to create a remarkable experience for our guests."

The most commonly made complaints about the Wizarding World of Harry Potter in Universal Studios Japan are about how crowded it is, how there are queues for everything, and how expensive it is.

Universal addressed the first of these problems by providing timed tickets. Many first-time guests suppose that once they have purchased their tickets at the main entrance they can just rush over to Hogsmeade and all is well. That rarely happens. What Universal has done is similar to the FastPass idea; guests are given timed tickets to let them know when they will be permitted into the Wizarding World. Once into Hogsmeade, guests should assume that every activity will require standing in line.

Unlike Tokyo Disneyland and Tokyo DisneySea, which have designated turnstiles, Universal Japan guests enter the park in a horde and once inside disperse to the various areas. As should be expected, the primary language used is Japanese and most of the team members and guests are locals. One exception are the Caucasian street performers. The rides are in Japanese as well, with dubbed voices on all the characters including the talking portraits and Moaning Myrtle in the bathrooms. Signage is primarily in English with Japanese in smaller text. Many of the team members are bilingual.

The entrance to the Wizarding World is marked by the Sundial Circle, or Sundial Garden, a circle of stone monuments not mentioned in the books, but first seen in *Harry Potter and the Prisoner of Azkaban*. It was here that Hermione punched Draco Malfoy and the trio later watched as Buckbeak was executed. Filmmakers created it to connect Hagrid's Hut to the castle.

After passing the stones, guests wander down a long winding path through the forest as music from the films drifts from hidden speakers. Signposts direct visitors past a slightly battered flying Ford Anglia and up to Hogsmeade gate, a replica of the entrance to the park in Orlando. The obvious difference between the two is that the one in Osaka has a small tower on the top of the stepped walls and the one in Orlando does not. The wording on the sign on both is in English. In the distance is Hogwarts Castle, made all the more spectacular than its Orlando cousin by the anticipatory journey toward it. The forest trail is the only way in and out of the Wizarding World which sets it apart from the Muggle world more effectively.

Also unique to Osaka is the tree-rimmed Black Lake, where Harry Potter and the other first years crossed in boats when they first arrived at Hogwarts. It was later the arrival point of the Durmstrang Institute ship and the location for the second task in the Triwizard Tournament in *Harry Potter and the Goblet of Fire*. Professor Dumbledore is buried on the shore.

Just inside the entrance to Hogsmeade is the Hogwarts Express with smoke wafting from its smokestack and steam coming from around the wheels. This version is static and appears to have emerged from a tunnel. There is a conductor for photo ops and to chat with and a laden baggage cart next to the locomotive at the top of a ramp. Not far away is a mockup of the inside of a passenger car where photos can be taken and purchased.

Similar shops, both real and façades, exist in both the Orlando and the Osaka parks. In alphabetical order. the façade shops are: Dogweed and Deathcap, purportedly selling exotic plants and flowers; J. Pippin's Potions, unique to Wizarding World Japan's Hogsmeade, selling "potions for all ailments," located over the Public Conveniences; Scrivenshafts Quill Shop, selling "finest parchments, inks and quills;" and Spintwitches, selling sporting goods and Quidditch supplies (in the front window façade is a Quidditch case in which the interactive wand will cause the quaffle and bludger to move); and Tomes and Scrolls, a specialist bookshop.

Guests can enter other shops and buy merchandise there.

Zonko's Joke Shop, a favorite place for Hogwarts students to shop as it was the purveyor of "jokes and tricks to fulfil even Fred and George Weasley's wildest dreams," sells such novelties as Dungbombs, Hiccough Sweets, Frog Spawn Soap, Sugar Quills, and Nose-biting Teacups.

Honeydukes sells Acid Pops, Bertie Bott's Every Flavour Beans, Cauldron Cakes, Exploding Bonbons, Fizzing Whizzbees, Chocolate Frogs with lenticular wizard cards, and other delicious treats. One of the longest lines in all of Hogsmeade Osaka isn't for Ollivanders or the Three Broomsticks, it's for Honeydukes.

Ollivanders wand shop contains "countless wand boxes stacked to the ceiling" and a unique interactive experience where a wand choses a wizard. Guests can purchase their own wand, collectible wand sets, or choose from a selection of film character wands. Unlike the Ollivanders in Orlando, there is a posted wait time for those wanting to enter the wand shop which could range from 10 minutes to an hour or more. The wizard conducting the show inside will use a combination of Japanese and English if Westerners are present.

Wiseacres Wizarding Equipment, a bright blue shop, welcomes all who wish to purchase wizarding equipment such as magnifying glasses, compasses, and binoculars, as well as a selection of ties and robes.

Behind Wiseacres is another gate with a "Welcome to Hogsmeade" sign with a walkway that leads to a quay out onto the lake. Upon closer investigation, bubbles can be seen rising from its dark and murky depths. Perhaps this is evidence of Merpeople, Grindylows, or the giant squid said to live within. According to Jo Rowling, the squid "is semi- domesticated and permits students to tickle its tentacles on sunny days, when it basks in the shadows."

On the opposite side of the street are the Owlery and the Owl Post where visitors can "send letters with a Hogsmeade postmark" or purchase stationery, writing implements, stamps, and owl-related toys and gifts. While all Wizarding Worlds have an Owl Post with animatronic owls decorating the rafters and walls, the Japan version also has live owls that caretakers carry around the park. None of the owleries in any of the parks resemble the Hogwarts Owlery nor is another such aviary mentioned in any of the books. The only resemblance is that the owl droppings are made from styrofoam dipped in plaster.

Dervish and Banges carries Spectrespecs, Quidditch equipment, Hogwarts uniforms, and more.

Gladrags Wizardwear, the shop with "a dress just like the one Hermione wore to the Yule Ball in the window," features fashion items and clothes as well as accessories and jewellery.

Filch's Emporium of Confiscated Goods, at the exit from Hogwarts, contains "items from caretaker Argus Filch's collection of treasures, confiscated from students of Hogwarts School."

The Butterbeer Cart often has queues as long as the queues for the attractions. At times a second cart is wheeled in to relieve the thirst of visitors.

Three Broomsticks is located by a small courtyard next to Honeydukes. Out front is a non-functioning but realistic-looking water pump and trough. This long-established tavern in Hogsmeade is favoured by teachers and students of Hogwarts. It serves traditional British dishes such as fish and chips and shepherd's pie as well as its specialty, Butterbeer. During the Christmas season, they sell hot Butterbeer.

Hog's Head, with a moving hog's head behind the counter, is "a dubious establishment adjacent to the Three Broomsticks" offering a broad selection of drinks, from Butterbeer to Hog's Head specially brewed draft beer.

The Frog Choir is composed of students from Hogwarts representing all four houses, Gryffindor, Slytherin, Hufflepuff, and Ravenclaw, presenting a "harmonic offering of songs...accompanied by their talented croaking frogs." Though not mentioned in the books, the Frog Choir, directed by Professor Flitwick, appeared in the film *Harry Potter and the Prisoner of Azkaban*.

In the same area is the new Wand Studios show that features four students from different Hogwarts Houses and teaches them wand mastery. The grand opening celebration showed off a bit of the wand class as visitors watched wizards and witches hone their skills.

The Triwizard Spirit Rally affords guests an opportunity to "cheer on a colorful procession of students from Beauxbatons and Durmstrang...and watch as they demonstrate their skill through enchanting performances." The stage is located just outside Hogsmeade Village on the way to the castle and is flanked by stone pillars and Hogwarts house banners.

The Flight of the Hippogriff, a Vekoma junior coaster, is longer and faster than its counterpart in Orlando. There are spaces for 16 riders in eight cars and children must be accompanied by an adult. Following a long queue, visitors pass by Hagrid's Hut with Sirius Black's motorcycle and sidecar parked outside and receive Hagrid's instructions on how to approach a hippogriff. The ride is approximately two minutes and provides aerial views of the park.

The only other ride attraction is Harry Potter and the Forbidden Journey which uses 4K3D state-of-the-art technology. This award-winning ride has been presented with the Golden Ticket Awards, Best Dark Ride Award 2013, and the 17th Annual Thea Outstanding Achievement Award.

Preceding the Forbidden Journey there is the Hogwarts Castle Walk that visitors can take without riding the attraction. The walkthrough queue is the same as in Orlando with the voices dubbed in Japanese, from the portraits to Dumbledore and Harry, Ron, and Hermione. Once completed the visitors simply exit the castle when they reach the Room of Requirement instead of carrying on to the ride.

For those brave souls who have decided to take the Forbiddden Journey, the same procedure as with the benches in Orlando is carried out. All packages being carried must be stashed in lockers before boarding. Because the Japanese are more motion-sensitive than Westerners, Universal Creative took pains to make this version of Harry Potter and the Forbidden Journey smoother and milder. Before installing the attraction in Osaka, it was test driven at Universal's Islands of Adventure in the Orlando park. Deemed a success, the smoother ride was then shipped to Japan to be installed. Except for being a less-exuberant ride and being dubbed in Japanese, the attraction is the same in Osaka and Orlando.

The Expecto Patronum Night Show was unveiled in mid-April 2017 with over 200 Potterphiles attending the preview performances, among them Saori Yoshida, a Potter fan and Olympic champion free-style wrestler. When asked about the show she said, "The Dementors made me so scared. It is absolutely the world's best experience." The show was run several times nightly and used projection mapping above Black Lake with Hogwarts Castle serving as the backdrop and focal point. The Expecto Patronum Night Show uses advanced video projection to bring Hogwarts Castle to life as students cast spells to illuminate the castle and Black Lake, and banish Dementors descending on the park. The Patronus Charm conjures a silvery phantom shape, usually that of an animal, which is the embodiment of the positive thoughts of the caster. A Patronus is effective in driving Dementors away. The interactive wand experience was also expanded to include the spells Aguamenti and Alohamora.

In March 2017, Comcast NBCUniversal took full ownership of Universal Studios Japan, paying $2.3 billion for the remaining 49 percent of shares. The transaction reflects an enterprise value of 840 billion yen ($7.4 billion US), including the assumption of debt.

The acquisition seems to have paid off as the number of visitors to Universal Studios Japan hit another record high for the third year in a row. In fiscal 2016, attendance rose by 700,000 from 2015 to 14.6 million. The rise is attributed to the new attractions, particularly in the Harry Potter area, and the events scheduled to celebrate the parks 15th year of operation. It was noticed at the same time that, on the same day, the Oriental Land Co., operator of Tokyo Disneyland and Tokyo Disney Sea, reported attendance down for the second consecutive year, though it should also be noted that combined attendance for those two parks was still over 30 million.

CHAPTER NINE
HARRY POTTER IN HOLLYWOOD

The Universal Film Manufacturing Company was founded by Carl Laemmle and several other people involved in the fledgling motion picture industry in April 1912. Their first studio was in Fort Lee, New Jersey, but moved to a 235-acre site in the San Fernando Valley of California in 1915. Here Laemmle opened the studio to the public, giving them a chance to see how movies were made. He charged 25 cents for the tour and added a chicken boxed lunch for another nickel. Though the Universal Studio tour provided additional income, the public soon became a nuisance when sound was added to the films. It was becoming increasingly difficult to keep the visitors quiet while shooting was in progress, so the tours were discontinued.

The studio remained closed to the public until 1961 when the lot reopened and tours were conducted by the Gray Line Bus Company. This worked for a time until Universal did a feasibility study and decided it would conduct its own tours.

Universal Studios Hollywood opened on July 15, 1964. In the first year, for $2.50 each, visitors clambered aboard the Glamor Trams for a ride around the backlot, stopping to see costumes, a makeup demonstration, a dressing room, and a western stunt show. Visitors could then purchase a meal at the studio commissary. The success of the venture led to an arena being built for the stunt show and the tour entrance being moved to the Upper Lot of Universal City where it is today.

In order to compete with the popularity of Disneyland in Anaheim, Universal started adding attractions to the tour. The first was a flash flood scene installed in 1968. The Parting of the Red Sea, as seen in *The Ten Commandments*, arrived in 1973; a collapsing bridge in 1974; and the Ice Tunnel in 1975.

These innovations boosted attendance, but it was the 25-foot animatronic shark from *Jaws*, based on Steven Spielberg's hit movie, that was to become the biggest attraction when added in 1976. The village of Amity helped round out the attacking shark scene and created a precedent for future attractions.

It would be another ten years before an even bigger attraction was added in the form of a 26,000-square foot soundstage featuring King Kong. Bob Gurr, who created many rides for Disneyland, built the animatronic gorilla, the largest in the world at the time. Two years later, in 1988, the tour trams would be shaken by a simulated 8.3 San Francisco tremor in Earthquake: The Big One.

Over the ensuing years Universal slowly evolved from a studio tour into a theme park as new attractions were added to the Upper Lot. In 1991, the Lower Lot was expanded and the two connected by a quarter-mile of escalators. E.T. Adventure was the park's first dark ride, opening at about the same time as the new Universal Studios Orlando park. This was auspicious, as the Florida park pointed the Universal Studios parks in a different direction.

CityWalk was added outside the gates in 1993 to provide a themed shopping and dining area. The focus was now on themed rides, with Back to the Future: The Ride replacing Battlestar Gallactica. Next came Jurassic Park: The Ride, The Land Before Time show, and T2 3D: Battle Across Time.

Over the next few years attractions opened and closed with regularity as Universal attempted to capitalize on current movie fads. Rugrats Magic Adventure replaced Totally Nickelodeon (2003), E.T. Adventure was transformed into Revenge of the Mummy: The Ride (2004); Fear Factor Live replaced Spider-Man Rocks (2005). In 2008 The Simpsons Ride and the Universal Story Museum opened and a year later Creature from the Black Lagoon: The Musical was swapped for Fear Factor Live in the Upper Lot. Transformers: The Ride arrived in 2010 along with King Kong 360 3-D.

Transformers opened on the Lower Lot in 2012 shortly before T2 3-D: Battle Across Time was closed and then replaced by Despicable Me: Minion Mayhem in 2014. Two other projects were also in the works: Springfield, built around a new Simpsons attraction, and, if rumors were true, Harry Potter.

The *Wall Street Journal* reported on December 1, 2011, that according to "people familiar with the matter," Universal Studios Hollywood was planning a Wizarding World of Harry Potter similar to that which opened in Orlando the year before. The report went on to state that similar additions were planned for Universal parks in Osaka, Singapore, and possibly Spain. Universal and Warner Bros. were negotiating a contract that was expected to be finalized within weeks.

It did not take Universal Studios Hollywood long before they acknowledged that plans for a Harry Potter attraction were underway. On December 6, 2011, Universal executives Tom Williams and Ron Meyer, along with executives from Warner Bros., California governor Jerry Brown, and James and Oliver Phelps announced the Wizarding World of Harry Potter was coming to Universal Studios Hollywood. There was very little announced beyond that. There were no details on what the Wizarding World would consist of, whether it would be a single attraction or a re-creation of what had been built in Orlando. It did become known that the Harry Potter area would replace the Gibson Amphitheatre, opened in 1972, and a re-creation of Hogwarts to contain Harry Potter and the Forbidden Journey was to be constructed.

That was the last the media heard about the project for almost two years. While West Coast Potterphiles waited for the Wizarding World to be built, the Gibson Amphitheater continued as usual until its final show in September 2013. "What's the hold up?" Potter fans wanted to know. Apparently, Universal had to wait for approval of their $1.6 billion, 25-year expansion proposal from the county board of supervisors. The project was touted as a great boon to tourism and the entertainment industry, as well as creating some 30,000 jobs during construction. Unanimous approval was granted by the board on April 23, 2013. Four months later, the Gibson closed and demolition could begin.

Security precautions were put in place to shield the project from prying eyes. A 24-hour guard was stationed on the soundstage where a replica of the Ford Anglia was being created. Only key members of Universal Creative or senior executives from Warner Bros., NBC, or Universal were given access.

In addition to the Wizarding World, Universal Creative was revamping much of the front half of the theme park in hopes of addressing the guest flow and visual confusion issues that had plagued the park. It was a massive project and would take more time than most Potterphiles had hoped to have to wait.

In June 2014, blogger Jim Hill reported on progress since his last visit the previous April: "It was clear that the construction crews…have made some huge progress." In September he reported: "Everywhere you look around Universal City, there are teams of construction workers taking down trees and/or trimming brush or building massive new parking structures. … Since I last walked about this construction fence, they've pushed it out a wee bit further." That meant the end of the fast-food stand with the Flintstones theme. Buildings in and round Hogsmeade were having sheet metal roofs installed along with the "underlying supports for many of the twisty chimneys that will sit on top of these structures." The massive Hogwarts Castle was also well underway with a walkway for workers "three or four stories off the ground…then an additional five or six stories of show building above that" and the towers and turrets still had to be added. All this in anticipation of the hordes of people expected to flood the new Wizarding World experience if what happened in Orlando was any indication.

Xiomara Wiley, senior vice-president of marketing and sales for Universal Studios Hollywood, announced in June 2015 that the Wizarding World of Harry Potter would open in spring 2016. She said that Harry Potter and the Forbidden Journey would be in Hogwarts and would "deliver a whole new level of hyper-realism when it has its U.S. debut with 3D HD technology" complete with Quidditch inspired 3D goggles. Also, Universal Hollywood's first outdoor roller coaster, Flight of the Hippogriff, would debut and there would be eight retail shops and two restaurants reflecting the magical wizarding world.

Another announcement was made in December 8, 2015, featuring Evanna Lynch. A firm opening date of April 7, 2016, was set, preceded by an unannounced soft opening on March 31.

The grand opening ceremony was held on a stage with Hogwarts Castles in the background. The Frog Choir started things off with "Something Wicked This Way Comes" followed by speeches by several Universal and Warner Bros. executives. Actors Evanna Lynch, Tom Felton, Warwick Davis, and arriving by flying Ford Anglia, James and Oliver Phelps. Special guest, composer and conductor John Williams, responsible for the scores of three of the films, was introduced and he conducted the Los Angeles Philharmonic through a medley of tunes from the films. Giant Slytherin snakes and Gryffindor lions crawled over the castle as the orchestra played and fireworks erupted in the night sky above the castle.

The Wizarding World of Harry Potter in Universal Studios Hollywood is a close copy of the Wizarding World in Orlando. There are some differences and subtle upgrades that will be mentioned later. Unlike Osaka's version, but similar to Islands of Adventure, there is no lead up to the Hogsmeade entrance; in Orlando visitors approach from the Lost Continent, in Hollywood they arrive at the entrance from Springfield, the home of the Simpsons, and Universal Plaza.

The entrance is the same as Orlando's was when it first opened, with the Hogwarts Express puffing steam just inside the stone arch. Nearby is a mock-up of a train cabin with actual movie props where visitors can have their pictures taken but "personal Muggle imaging devices" are not permitted. The set is familiar in every detail, even using the actual luggage racks from the films. "Wherever we can find the real thing, we will," art director Alan Gilmore said, "and if we can't find the real thing, we'll replicate it."

Hogsmeade is as exquisite in detail here as elsewhere, with the cobble streets; steeply pitched, snow-covered, slate roofs; multi-paned, bowed windows; bright colors; tall, crooked chimneys; and gables.

Honeydukes is the first shop. It offers a selection of treats and sweets, from Acid Pops to Fizzing Whizzbees and a bakery inside offering Cauldron Cakes and Chocolate Frogs. The sweet shop was one of the highlights for students from Hogwarts on their visits to Hogsmeade. Shelf after peppermint-green and cotton-candy-pink shelf tempted the sweet tooth of many youngsters. Here was everything, from Skeleton Pops and Exploding Bons-Bons to Liquorice Wands and Lima's Crazy Blob Drops, mostly invented by the props department. On set, each sweet had its own labeling and distinctive boxes, and actors were informed before shooting started that the treats were coated with lacquer to keep them from spoiling. As it happened, this was untrue; it was simply a ruse to stop the children from eating all the props.

Zonko's Joke Shop, despite its impressive façade, is just the back wall of Honeydukes selling "jokes and tricks to fulfil even Fred and George Weasley's wildest dreams." They have Dungbombs (magical stink bombs, banned from Hogwarts), Nose-Biting Teacups, Sugar Quills, Hiccup Sweets, Frog Spawn Soap, and a selection of Pygmy Puffs and Fanged Flyers. Some of these were mentioned in the books and some were invented by the designers.

Set back from the main street is the Three Broomsticks, slightly larger than its Orlando counterpart, selling British staples such as fish and chips, Shepherd's Pie, Bangers and Mash, Guinness Stew, Pumpkin Juice, and Butterbeer. It also has an expanded menu and includes items from Orlando's Leaky Cauldron. Another interesting difference is that there is no Hot Butterbeer or Butterbeer Ice Cream at the Hollywood Three Broomsticks, yet. It hosts one of the new interactive wand sites, featuring a poster of Sirius Black.

The Hog's Head tavern is at the rear, a full-service bar that offers specialty brews such as Hog's Head Brew, Wizard's Brew, Dragon Scale, Authentic Fire Whisky, wine, domestic and imported beers, mixed drinks, and Butterbeer. Of all the beverages served in Wizarding World parks, only Pumpkin Juice and Butterbeer are mentioned in the books.

Next is Ollivanders Wand Shop where a brief show matches wizard or witch to wand. Though located in Diagon Alley in the books and films, this Ollivanders is a branch office of the original, placed here through dispensation from J.K. Rowling. This version was expanded upon when the shop in Orlando received higher-than-anticipated crowds. Up to 24 guests can be wedged in to witness the show where the wand chooses the wizard.

There are two separate choosing chambers and a shaded queue making it seem more of an attraction than a shop.

The wand selection show happens every few minutes (a clock counts down to the next one) as a random guest, often a child in Hogwarts regalia, is chosen to take part in the wand-choosing ceremony. The Wandkeeper looks the participant over, selects a wand, and urges them to give it a try. The person attempts the spell, often with unexpected and amusing results, and eventually, lights, wind, and special effects occur to indicate the wand has chosen the wizard or witch.

The interactive wands available here can be used at designated areas around Hogsmeade to cause items in various locations, indicated by medallions in front of shops, to perform. A map is provided to show the locations, and wands from Orlando work here as well. Battery recharging and repairs at Ollivanders are included in the price. Hollywood's Ollivanders is located on the other side of High Street from the one in Orlando.

Adjacent is Wiseacre's Wizarding Equipment where wands can be purchased without the show. Visitors will also find "house robes, Platform 9¾ train station items, Hogwarts Express items, and a variety of wizarding wares and supplies, including crystal balls, telescopes, binoculars, armillary spheres." Wisecare's did not exist in the original Orlando Hogsmeade, but was added to Diagon Alley when it was built. There is an interactive wand site here where a flick of the wand will open a small chest of drawers in the window.

Across the street is the Owlery providing benches in the shade. In the timber rafters of the arched ceilings are nearly two dozen resting owls dozing, hooting, turning their heads, and ruffling their feathers. There is a howler display and a grand Owlery clock hoots the hour. Postcards and letters can be mailed here and delivered with a Hogwarts postmark. The Owl Post sells stationery and writing implements, including quills, and Wizarding World of Harry Potter stamps, as well as owl-related toys and gifts.

Dervish and Banges is a magic supply shop selling brooms and Quidditch equipment such as t-shirts, quaffles, Golden Snitches, and brooms including the Nimbus 2001 and the

Firebolt. There are also magical items such as Spectrespecs and *The Monster Book of Monsters*, along with the latest in wizarding fashion and school robes. The shop is located on a new, short street, dubbed Town Wall by Alan Gilmore. The street is primarily façades, so there are interesting window displays and one of the interactive wand sites. The Magic Neep, a magical green grocer, is one of the storefronts along Town Wall. Though not in any of the books or films, it does appear in *Fantastic Beasts: Cases from the Wizarding World*, the mobile hidden object game available on Android and iOS devices. In addition to the widening of the main Hogsmeade road, this new street was intended to be more accommodating for large crowds.

In the front window of Gladrags Wizardwear, guests will see Hermione's Yule Ball gown. Inside is Cho Chang's gown and many of the fabrics and buttons used in the making of the costumes. The shop sells a variety of fashionable wizard wear such as authentic wizards' robes and accessories and other apparel and jewelry fashion items inspired by the four school houses. Gladrags also has shops in Osaka, Paris, and London, but not in the Orlando Hogsmeade. It was here that Harry Potter bought socks for Dobby, "including a pair patterned with flashing gold and silver stars, and another that screamed loudly when they became too smelly."

Filch's Emporium of Confiscated Goods is at the exit from Hogwarts Castle where all manner of Harry Potter-themed merchandise is available. Souvenirs like plush toys, caps, t-shirts, jackets, sweatshirts, bags, pins, jewelry, collectibles, keychains, glassware, travel accessories, stationery, books. and numerous other items are available.

One striking difference between Orlando and Hollywood is the background, over which Universal has no control. In Hollywood one can see mountains in the distance, substituting for the Scottish Highlands, whereas Orlando is flat. "I think this is my favorite setting," notes Alan Gilmore. "The environment works with the world. One side is like Scottish Highlands, the other is an English village." Also, because of the way Hogsmeade is situated, buildings from other areas of the park can be seen between the pointed roofs. Gilmore and his team have attempted to distract guests' eyes from these intrusions by adding more detail to what they want them to see. "Little nuances have been tweaked," Gilmore says. "We designed it very much for the light in California. The light in L.A. is so pure, it really helped me refine the detailing and textures and colors."

The showcase windows have more details and the interactive wand areas have been upgraded. There are eleven locations marked with a subtle seal on the ground for interactive wands. "J.K. Rowling helped us create the spells," Gilmore said. "We worked with her to add these extra layers to create a seamless journey, from the books to the films to the parks."

The Flight of the Hippogriff is to the right of the castle and has a winding path leading up to the attraction. Hagrid's Hut can be seen here with Fang barking inside and Hagrid giving instructions. Once on the attraction, guests have the opportunity to bow to Buckbeak before being whisked around the one-minute roller-coaster ride. This version travels slightly higher, moves a bit faster, and is a smoother, more modern Mack YoungSTAR coaster instead of the repurposed Vekoma Junior used in Orlando.

As in the other Wizarding Worlds, Harry Potter and the Forbidden Journey is the highlight of this park. Similar to Orlando and Osaka, the ride is preceded by an entertaining walkthrough. Passing through the Winged Boar gates, guests move toward Hogwarts at varying speeds, depending on the time of day and how busy it is. The Weasley's badly battered Ford Anglia is found on a rocky outcropping in an expanded outdoor queue as there is no Dragon Challenge queue for it here. The locker room provided for guests to stow anything they can't take on the ride is larger and more spacious than its equivalent in Orlando.

Once inside the castle guests walk through various props from the films and eventually emerge outside in the Hogwarts greenhouses where much of the winding queue is located. Other than an occasional mandrake, there is little to see here. Once back inside again, there is the hall of portraits including the founders of Hogwarts, Godric Gryffindor, Helga Hufflepuff, Salazar Slytherin, and Romena Ravenclaw. The four are arguing about Quidditch and Dumbledore's decision to allow Muggles inside the castle. Next is the headmaster's office where Dumbledore speaks to visitors though a high-definition video projection system called Musion Eyeliner technology. He then sends guests on their way to the Defence Against the Dark Arts classroom to hear a history of Hogwarts lecture by Professor Binns, the professor who is a ghost but does not know it.

Harry, Ron, and Hermione appear from under the cloak of invisibility while guests wait for the lecture and offer them a way out of the boring subject. They suggest that a guided tour of Hogwarts and a Quidditch match would be more fun. Due to the cavernous nature of some of the rooms and the fact that the lines are spoken with an English accent of varying degrees of intelligibility, some American Muggles might have difficulty understanding what is being said. Guests then enter the Gryffindor Common Room for instructions and then the Room of Requirement to board the ride.

The seats are benches attached to a KOKA robotic arm much like those used in auto assembly plants. Initially, this version of the ride was in 3D HD and visitors wore Quidditch-style goggles. Other changes were the sizes of the interior sets, becoming larger in Hollywood; the sound effects and lighting were also ramped up. The Dementor army was expanded and their arms stretched out farther than those in Orlando.

Before installing Harry Potter and the Forbidden Journey in Hollywood, the team went back to the film and added new 3D elements by enhancing the older shots. The dragon in the first scene appeared to come much closer to the riders. Coup Thierry said: "We did the same thing with the snitch in the Quidditch match. Also, the Dementors…now get right up in your face and you can feel their breath."

Universal Creative also added more sets, scenes, and detailing to the castle. The Forbidden Forest was expanded and more sets were added to the Chamber of Secrets to, as Thierry stated, "raise the bar one more time. With the changes that we made to the Hollywood version of this attraction, we were hoping that we could turn it into the ultimate immersive experience." There were audio enhancements as well, and a scorekeeper was added for the Quidditch match along with more Dementors.

Before long it was found that, despite the hype, not everything was an improvement over the Orlando original. The film footage was the same, shot in 2008, but when converted to 3D some of the sequences were blurred and oversaturated. This tended to make the aggressive movements even more nauseating for many riders. Unfortunately, Hogwarts Hollywood does not have a castle-only tour for guests want to do the entertaining queue without taking the stomach-churning ride. There is, however, what has been termed a secret room, where guests who "feel like they've swallowed too much Gilyweeed" and are feeling a little sick can have a few moments to themselves.

In December, eight months after the opening of Harry Potter and the Forbidden Journey, the 3D special effect was removed, making the Hollywood version the same as the Orlando attraction. Without announcement, park workers stopped distributing 3D glasses to guests and reverted the projected videos in the ride to standard 2D images. Officials offered no explanation for the change, stating only that "we continually evaluate our theme park ride experiences, and enabling our guests to enjoy Forbidden Journey without the use of 3D is one example of how we are assessing various opportunities."

Guests and theme park insiders speculated that the change was due to the high instances of nauseated riders. Many reported enjoying the ride more without the 3D effects removed. Even though other rides use similar technology, the additional tilting and lifting of the seats seemed to have added to the sensation in a less-than-positive manner.

More changes were on the way. Less than four months after the removal of the 3D effect, a new innovative technology was introduced. Whereas the images were originally projected on the wraparound screens in 3D and at 60 frames per second, the new upgrade was to 120 frames per second with a horizontal resolution of about 4000 pixels in high definition. The technology was described as state-of-the-art 4K-HD. Audrey Eig, a park spokesperson explained: "As a progressive theme park, we determined the increased frame rate would offer an even more intense and immersive experience for our guests."

In addition to enhancing Harry Potter and the Forbidden Journey, other aspects of the park were also tweaked before being rebuilt in Hollywood. According to Stuart Craig: "Since we built the first Wizarding World in Orlando, some of our production and design techniques have been richly enhanced, which is why we decided to change the way that the snow sits on the roofs out here in Hollywood. We wanted things to look as real as they possibly could in this version of Hogsmeade, which is why we even changed the way we formed the icicles that hang down from so many of the village's rooftops and window sills."

California's strong sunlight also influenced the changes that were made by Universal Creative in Hollywood. "The quality of light here in southern California is amazing. It's so vivid. It almost feels like hi-def when you look at objects here. As we were designing the Wizarding World for Universal Studios Hollywood, we knew that we had to take the almost unforgiving quality of that sunlight into account, which is why we enhanced a lot of the colors and the textures that we used on the West Coast version of Hogwarts Castle and Hogsmeade so that they'd then look as good as they should in this particular setting," art director Alan Gilmore said, pointing out that in Florida, the walls have a satin finish, whereas he chose glossy paint in Hollywood to better reflect and accent the light.

In describing the differences between the parks, Gilmore also noted: "There's an extra level of patina. The grime tells the story of the history. It all feels very natural, organic, and comfortable, and that's deliberate." Stuart Craig added: "It's a big feature here where everything is usually clean. We have black soot, moss, stains, and rust. It was fun to explore that and extend it to get the most value out of it in this park."

When the Hollywood version was being designed in the fall of 2010, the design team in London built models, both physical and computer, of the terrain around Universal Studios. Gilmore said: "We actually designed views to take advantage of the way this version of the castle would sit up in the Hollywood Hills…for example, when the queue for Forbidden Journey passes through the space where Madam Sprout teaches her herbology classes. As guests move through those greenhouses at the back of the castle, they're going to get this lovely view of the nearby mountain tops."

The interior queue was also plussed by placing in the classroom "the actual desks from that set. And the chalkboard in there is the original chalkboard as well," Gilmore said. "Universal Creative's prop team has made props of such high quality that they blend seamlessly with the film props."

The popularity of the opening ceremony show in the spring when John Williams conducted an orchestra playing his famous Harry Potter music accompanied by light projection and fireworks was not lost on park officials. Tim Runco, senior vice president of entertainment, remarked: "We spent a lot of time figuring out how to bring that out in a way so that's it not just playing to you. 'Immersive' is really an overused word, but we really did bring people into it."

The result appeared that summer. As night fell, the words of the Sorting Hat were projected over Hogsmeade: "There's nothing I can't see, so try me on and I will tell you where you ought to be." Following was a five-minute spectacular with images of the Hogwarts houses flitted over the mountain top castle. The music was recorded at Abbey Road's legendary Studio One by the London Symphony Orchestra. Each instrument was recorded individually with a multi-channel system, eight models of speakers, and 3-D projection mapping, giving guests a different view depending on where they stood to view the show. The audio was piped in through a 27.5 surround-sound system. Runco continued: "People have such a strong connection to this story. With the music, you don't want to detract from it, you want to amplify it because it's so amazing."

One of the worst-kept secrets in the theme park world is that Universal Studios Hollywood is planning to expand their Wizarding World to include the Diagon Alley expansion in Universal Studios Orlando that opened in the summer of 2014. Rumours abound as to what it will entail and where it will be located. One possible plan is to use the Hogwarts Express concept introduced in Orlando to take guests from Hogsmeade on the Upper Lot down to Diagon Alley on the Lower Lot.

Another plan, according to a *Los Angeles Times* source, was that the expansion would place Diagon Alley on the site of the current Waterworld stunt show. This raises the question as to the necessity of the Hogwarts Express attraction with Hogsmeade located right next to the Waterworld area. It has also been suggested that "if Hollywood's version of Diagon Alley included the Hogwarts Express, it might not actually move anywhere. The Hogwarts Express experience would be similar to what guests experience in Orlando, but the train wouldn't actually move, with guests exiting out of the other side of the train to arrive in Diagon Alley." This attraction could be enhanced with simulated movements and special effects.

The 2017 LIMA International Licensing Awards took place during the Licensing Expo at the Mandalay Bay Convention Center in Las Vegas, with winners spanning 20 categories. The Wizarding World of Harry Potter—Hogsmeade at Universal Studios Hollywood took home the prize for location-based or experiential initiative.

As shown in the past, Universal is seldom anxious to reveal future plans, often waiting until after construction has actually begun to do so. The plans to expand the Wizarding World of Harry Potter Hollywood with a Diagon Alley are said to be locked in for a 2020 opening, which could develop into an interesting competition with Disneyland's new Star Wars Land.

Jack Warner, one of the famous Warner brothers, enjoyed showing friends and guests around his studio. Though he sometimes had mail room employees perform the task, he was opposed to opening the studio to the public, as Carl Laemmle had with his Universal Studios, fearing the distraction would interfere with studio production. One of the most popular tour guides was a mail room employee named Dick Mason. His knowledge of the studio led to Jack assigning him to assist his vice president of worldwide production.

It wasn't until Jack Warner retired in 1969 that serious thought was given to establishing a studio tour of Warner Bros. Studio. In 1971, when financial hardship plagued the company, Warner Bros. signed a deal with struggling Columbia Pictures to combine and create the Burbank Studios. To increase revenue a tour department, managed by Dick Mason, was established. Three dollars and an advance reservation were required to book a tour.

Initially, Mason had seven tour guides and limited the tours to twelve people at one time. The guides' spiels were unscripted and the tour depended upon what areas were available; generally the sound stages, backlot, and prop house were included. Popularity spread by word of mouth and before long the tour, four times a day for about three hours, was bringing in 15,000 visitors each year.

Mason was only interested in educating, not entertaining, the public. Unlike Universal's Studio tour, there were no special effects shows or simulations. "We just want to give insight to a business most people have misunderstands about," Mason told the *Milwaukee Journal*.

Warner Bros. reclaimed the studio from Columbia in the 1990s and the tour department was relocated next to Gate 4 on Hollywood Way, sharing space with the studio store. Dick Mason retired in 2000 and his role was assumed by Danny Kahn who moved the office across the street to Gate 5. Kahn began an aggressive advertising campaign for the studio tour and increased the number of daily tours, but kept the groups small and the spiels unscripted.

The tour was rebranded in 2015 with a new name, logo, and tour carts when Stage 48: Script to Screen was launched. The tour is now known as Warner Bros. Studio Tour Hollywood (previously Warner Bros. Studios VIP Tour) to identity it more closely with the successful Warner Bros. Studio Tour London. Today there are two tours, the deluxe tour lasting 5 or 6 hours and a standard tour of 2 or 3 hours. As in the original tours, each differs according to availability of sites, but each includes a visit to at least one soundstage with a show in production but not filming; a look at the backlot to view various sets, entrance to the archive which presently features Harry Potter props and costumes, a garage containing cars used in various Warner Bros. films, the prop house, and Stage 48: Script to Screen, a self-guided interactive soundstage that takes visitors through the film production process. In the post-production section of Stage 48 is a green screen area with a Harry Potter twist where guests can watch themselves fly on a Firebolt or Nimbus 2000 through London's busy streets. There is also a screen showing how motion capture is done, using Dobby as an example.

The day before the new and expanded Harry Potter exhibit opened to the public, on December 5, 2016, Warner Bros. Studio Tour Hollywood invited special guests Dan Fogler (Jacob Kowalski) and Bonnie Wright (Ginny Weasley) as representatives of both the Fantastic Beasts and Harry Potter film series to tour its latest addition. Originally dedicated solely to Harry Potter, the reimagined exhibit now offered a look at props from both Fantastic Beasts as well.

Harry Potter and the Fantastic Beasts exhibit was designed to guide visitors on a quick tour of the process, from concept art to finished movie. At the entrance to the exhibit is a case containing Harry Potter's iconic glasses, the acceptance letter from Hogwarts, and his wand. One wall is covered with artwork of scenes from the films, and scattered about are various props from the Harry Potter films such as a case full of Weasley's Whizzing Wheezes, the Marauders' Map, a full-sized figure of Dobby the house-elf, and pages from *The Quibbler* and *The Daily Prophet*.

The costumes of Molly and Arthur Weasley are displayed in front of a painting of their home, the Burrow. In front of a painting of the Dark Lord are the costumes of young Tom Riddle as worn when he resided in an orphanage, his Hogwarts uniform, and Voldemort's shapeless robes showing the evolution from a nasty child to an even nastier Dark Lord. Voldemort's wand is in a case nearby. A large Gryffindor house crest is the front for various styles of house uniforms as they evolved through the films.

There is a Sorting Hat and stool placed in front on an exhibit of costumes where guests can take part in a Sorting Hat ceremony. When Bonnie Wright and Dan Fogler toured the exhibit prior to opening, they were both sorted into Gryffindor. The raised dais behind is reminiscent of a portion of the Great Hall with dragon-shaped lantern holders flanking the stage. The costumes include professors Minerva McGonagall, Albus Dumbledore, and Severus Snape as well as Groundskeeper Rubeus Hagrid and the post *Harry Potter and the Prisoner of Azkaban* version of Professor Filius Flitwick.

The newest addition to the exhibit highlights *Fantastic Beasts and Where to Find Them*. Featured are the costumes worn by Eddie Redmayne (Newt Scamander), Katherine Waterston (Tina Goldstein), Alison Sudol (Queenie Goldstein), Dan Fogler (Jacob Kowalski), and Colin Farrell (Percival Graves).

Danny Kahn, executive director of Warner Bros. Studio Tour Hollywood, introduced the exhibit by saying: "We are excited to let the world peer behind the lens to see how filmmakers develop the entertainment we love. This experience will transport guests from Harry Potter's Hogwarts adventures back to 1926 New York, where Newt Scamander's misplaced magical case has found its home."

There is a scene with a New York Port Authority background with different types of luggage. This was where Newt arrived in America with his suitcase full of magical creatures.

Another of the scenes from *Fantastic Beasts* features part of the Jacob's bedroom set in his apartment. The backdrop shows the wall blown out, a fire escape, and a clothesline-draped New York skyline. Newt's magical suitcase in on the unmade bed and the costume of Jacob Kowalski, worn by Dan Folger, is nearby. On a table at the head of the bed is Jacob's open suitcase containing a selection of pastries he had taken to the bank in his effort to secure a loan to open a bakery. According to Stuart Craig, the apartment was "copied in quite a disciplined and deliberate way" from a re-creation he had seen in the Tenement Museum. He thought it was "absolutely ideal for the character of Jacob and his situation: the smallness, the relative poverty in which he lived."

A sign with the words "Kowalski Quality Bakery Goods" highlights a Lower East Side street scene from the end of the film. This is where Jacob had set up his long-desired bakery after Newt gave him some Occamy eggshells to sell for the necessary funds. A bakery cart contains four or five different pastries designed by Kowalski based on his subconscious memories of the beasts he encountered while involved with Newt Scamander. Pierre Bohanna pointed out that "we had guys replicate Erumpents and Murtlaps as pastries," but "they didn't do them for real, they were synthetic, but they looked nice." After he got the part for the film, Dan Fogler's father told him that his great-grandfather had been a baker, a fact Fogler had not previously known.

The MACUSA (Magical Congress of the United States of America) seal is on the floor in front of a section devoted to the American version of Britain's Ministry of Magic. The MACUSA logo was the first thing created by graphic designers and features a phoenix and the 48 star, 1926 version of the American flag with some of the stars breaking away. There are newspapers on the wall beside the costume of Percival Graves (Colin Farrell) and a few artifacts in a case, including Graves' wand and an identification card. The backdrop is of the interior of the MACUSA headquarters. The interior set for MACUSA had been constructed on M Stage at Leavesden. Craig had envisioned a massive railway station concourse with forty-foot high gilded phoenixes and decked out in black, gold, emerald, and maroon with "little touches of magic."

The costumes worn by Tina and Queenie Goldstein in the speakeasy scene are against a backdrop of the Blind Pig. The subterranean speakeasy was run by a goblin named Gnarlak. Dark and dingy, it is the favoured hangout of the less-than-savory denizens of the wizard world in New York. Here would be found giants, goblins, house elves, and assorted ne'er-do-well wizard folk. Tina and Queenie magically changed from their street clothes into more fashionable "flapper" attire before entering the club. Newt merely changed his neckwear to a bowtie.

CHAPTER TEN

THE REST OF THE WIZARDING WORLD

The Harry Potter Shop at Platform 9¾

The Harry Potter Shop at Platform 9¾ opened its doors to the public at King's Cross Station in London on December 15, 2012. The shop was opened by Warwick Davis, who played both Professor Flitwick and the goblin Griphook in the films. Surrounded by crowds of Harry Potter fans, Warwick read a brief speech and cut a ribbon to declare the shop open.

When asked what he would like from the shop, he replied he wouldn't mind "a functioning Deluminator to save him the trouble of turning the lights off at night." When asked which character to preferred to play, Griphook or Flitwick, he decided on "both of them."

The shop is under license from Warner Bros. and is produced by Jonathan Sands, founder and chief executive of the London Film Museum, and partners. In an interview before the launch, Sands said: "This is precisely where Harry's journey to Hogwarts began. King's Cross Station has recently undergone the most amazing re-development and we are delighted to be a part of it, thanks to Network Rail."

Every effort was made to keep the construction and eventual use of the shop quiet to prevent spoiler photography. Both employees and promotors were successful; even the most watchful fan sites were unaware of it until shortly before opening day.

The shop is reminiscent of the shops in the Wizarding Worlds, small and packed with merchandise. The usual wands, plush toys, keychains, sweaters, scarves, jewelry, Noble collection items, prints, and books are present.

Outside a cast iron plaque reading 'Platform 9¾' was installed in 1999 in a passageway between the main station and the annex containing platforms 9 to 11. Beneath the sign the rear of a baggage trolley protrudes from the brick wall which quickly became a popular photo spot for travelers. The display was revamped to include luggage and a birdcage and moved in 2012 with the development of the new concourse building and placed closer to the Harry Potter Shop.

When *Harry Potter and the Philosopher's Stone* was shot, St. Pancras station, being more attractive, was used instead of King's Cross. J.K. Rowling, when placing the scene in her book, misremembered the platform numbering and described the station incorrectly. In fact, as Stuart Craig explained, "Platforms 9 and 10 are not in the main station building, but in a little annex to the side." For the purposes of the film Platform 9¾ was shot between Platforms 4 and 5, much to the delight of passersby who gathered around after they noticed the Hogwarts Express and film crew.

Legoland

Previously, in May 2009, J.K. Rowling had been memorialized in a Lego mosaic at Legoland Windsor. The tribute contained 48,000 white, grey, and yellow bricks, and was put together with the aid of children who had voted Rowling most worthy of the honor. Vicky Brown, general manager of Legoland Windsor said: "We are thrilled that J.K. Rowling topped this poll as her books have been a great inspiration to children of all ages. At Legoland, we actively encourage imagination and creativity and believe in making the children the heroes just as Rowling does in her stories." Other notables who ranked in the Legoland poll were Daniel Radcliffe, Sir David Attenborough, and then U.S. president Barack Obama.

An experiment happened on the other side of the Atlantic at Legoland in California where a Harry Potter overlay had been installed on the Hideaways area and full-sized Harry Potter characters were created out of Lego bricks. Many Lego Stores displayed these life-sized figures.

Illustrating Harry Potter

From March 23, 2017, until late June, the Baliffgate Museum in Alnwick showcased models, original illustrations, sketches, and final prints from the new edition of J.K. Rowling's *Harry Potter and the Philosophers Stone*, illustrated by Jim Kay.

The museum's new Illustrating Harry Potter exhibition broke all attendance records at the venue. The exhibition was put together by Seven Stories, the National Centre for Children's Books in Newcastle, and Bloomsbury Children's Books. Most of the early visitors were Potterphiles and some came in Hogwarts uniform. Some of the early scenes outside Hogwarts Castle in the first two films were shot at Alnwick Castle.

J.K. Rowling had personally selected Jim Kay to do the artwork in the republished illustrated hardcover editions. "I love his interpretation of Harry Potter's world and I feel honoured and grateful that he has lent his talent to it," she said. Kay plans to do the entire seven-volume set.

The museum exhibit featured intricate sketches and pencil drawings that visitors could examine to discover Kay's creative process, from inspiration to the final illustration. Included are Kay's model of the Hogwarts Express, artwork of many the main characters, and a brief film that Kay made showing him working on the illustrations for *Harry Potter and the Chamber of Secrets* in his small studio office at the rear of his home.

The view Kay has of his garden provided inspiration for many of his sketches. His illustrations in Patrick Ness' book *A Monster Calls* earned him the 2012 Kate Greenaway Medal.

His preferred medium for the Harry Potter books is watercolor and pencil which he uses to great effect to add rich detail and humour to the books that perfectly complements Rowling's works.

Harry Potter: A History of Magic

The British Museum announced on March 31, 2017, their plans for a Harry Potter exhibition to be called Harry Potter: A History of Magic that would begin on October 20, 2017.

The exhibition was in celebration of the 20th anniversary of the publication of *Harry Potter and the Philosopher's Stone* on June 26, 1997. The museum went beyond the Harry Potter stories and included "everything from rare books, manuscripts and treasures from the British Library's archives to original drafts and drawings from J.K. Rowling."

Amongst the original material from Rowling was a handwritten draft of the Sorting Hat song from *Harry Potter and the Philosopher's Stone*. The words are identical to those found in the book except for the ninth line that Rowling scratched out and omitted from the finished song.

Julian Harrison, lead curator of Medieval Historical Manuscripts at the British Library and lead curator of the Harry Potter exhibition, said: "It's always so thrilling to see an author's original draft in their own handwriting, and J.K. Rowling's draft of the Sorting Hat song is no exception. It's integral to the Harry Potter stories, and it's amazing to see how it was originally written and amended. We hope this provides an exciting taster of what kind of material visitors can expect to see in our exhibition."

The curators selected numerous stories from the museum holdings of history and mythology to illustrate what lies behind modern magical traditions. Over 100 artifacts went on display, some from the British Museum, others on loan from institutions across the globe. In addition, there was new material from Rowling and her publisher, Bloomsbury.

A preparatory sketch of a mandrake made by Jim Kay for the illustrated edition of *Harry Potter and the Chamber of Secrets* was included along with other pieces of his art. Original manuscripts and editorial notes from the publisher were also on display.

Defence Against the Dark Arts, Divination, Care of Magical Creatures, and Potions each had a room in the exhibition that was devoted to a different class from the Hogwarts curriculum. To complement the fiction pieces were illustrated manuscripts such as *Splendor Solis* (Splendour of the Sun), written in Germany in 1582 and containing an illustration of an alchemist in red and blue robes and wearing a red hat. It was suggested that this was something like what Nicolas Flamel, co-creater of the Philosopher's Stone, might have worn.

As part of the Potions section Harrison introduced other examples showing some early depictions of magic from the British Library's collections. One was from 1480 and is the first known depiction of a witch's cauldron from the book *On Witches and Female Fortune Tellers* by Ulrich Molitor and shows "two elderly women placing a snake and a cockerel respectively into a large flaming pot, in order to create a hailstorm." A second image from 1491 shows an old potions master titled *A Potions Class* from the text *Ortus Sanitatis* (The Garden of Health). The master is wearing an ermine-lined green cloak.

Other pieces included medieval imagery of dragons and a 13th century image of a phoenix rising from the ashes for the Care of Magical Creatures section. "We had to have some dragons!" Harrison quipped. "In the past, some of these fantastic beasts were even believed to be real. In ancient times, they would try to work out how to kill a basilisk, and one of the ways was to confront it with a weasel. Apparently weasel scent or urine was fatal to basilisks. If Harry Potter had known this, he would've had a weasel in his pocket!"

A Celebration of Harry Potter

A Celebration of Harry Potter was held at Universal Studios Orlando from January 24-26, 2014. Tickets sold out within minutes of the announcement being made the previous August.

Celebrations began with a tribute to Harry Potter on the Music Plaza Stage, the park's main live performance venue. The artist who reimagined the Harry Potter 15th anniversary covers for Scholastic, Kazu Kibuishi, was on hand to autograph copies of the Harry Potter books. Paul Harris, the wand combat choreographer for *Harry Potter and the Order of the Phoenix*, and Mark Williams (Arthur Weasley) were sponsored by Warner Bros. Studio Tour Leavesden. Harris gave lessons in defensive and offensive wand techniques and dueled with select members from the audience.

Present at a panel discussion were designers Eduardo Lima and Miraphora Mina of MinaLima, who established the visual graphic style of the Harry Potter films. Tom Hodgson, Pottermore's creative director, was also on hand to present artwork from the special edition of *Harry Potter and the Goblet of Fire* and play an exclusive audio clip of J.K. Rowling giving the backstory of Professor Gilderoy Lockhart.

There was a Props panel discussion about bringing Harry Potter magic to the theme parks with Alan Gilmore (art director), Aaron Baker (senior prop manager), and Bryn Court (film sculptor). Fans' questions were addressed with a cast question-and-answer panel composed of Evanna Lynch (Luna Lovegood), James and Oliver Phelps (Fred and George Weasley), Matthew Lewis (Neville Longbottom), and Devon Murray (Seamus Finnigan).

Harry Potter: The Exhibition also had a Harry Potter expo with movie props on display. Matthew Lewis made a surprise appearance at, and assisted in, the Sorting Hat ceremony.

With the obvious success of the first A Celebration of Harry Potter, Universal Studios made it an annual event. The second was held from January 30 to February 1, 2015, and also sold out quickly.

Opening night was repeated on the Music Plaza Stage with Sir Michael Gambon (Albus Dumbledore), Evanna Lynch, and James and Oliver Phelps on hand for a brief introduction. Battle Like a Durmstrang and Dance Like a Beauxbatons classes were held, and the Hogwarts Frog Choir performed their famous "Something Wicked This Way Comes" number. Wand master Paul Harris returned for dueling demonstrations with special duelist Evanna Lynch assisting with guest and audience duels.

MinaLima and Kazu Kibuishi participated in panel discussions again and at the end of the first night Sir Michael Gambon, Evanna Lynch, James Phelps, and Oliver Phelps participated in a question-and-answer session with the media. Afterward, the cast members were available for autograph signings. Harry Potter film trivia, house photo opportunities, and watching a movie in the park on the Music Plaza Stage filled the rest of the weekend.

The third annual A Celebration of Harry Potter was announced for January 29 to 31, 2016. At the Music Plaza Stage show were Rupert Grint (Ron Weasley), Bonnie Wright (Ginny Weasley), Katie Leung (Cho Chang), Matthew Lewis, and Evanna Lynch. Both Muggles and Wizards paid tribute to the late Alan Rickman (Severus Snape). Exclusive scenes from *Fantastic Beasts and Where to Find Them* and *Harry Potter and the Cursed Child* were shown on the big screen. Evanna Lynch and Pottermore shared details of Wizarding Schools around the globe. At the end of opening night everyone present was encouraged to point their wands skyward and shout "Lumos Maxima" to fill the night sky with a fireworks display.

In addition to the now customary appearances of the design team of MinaLima and wand master Paul Harris was Pierre Bohanna, prop maker for the Harry Potter films. Bohanna and Matt Lewis showcased Harry Potter Props and discussed Newt Scamander's wand. Attendees were encouraged to write on Scholastic's Muggle Wall. There was a wand making demonstration and a huge map showing the locations of the worldwide Wizarding Schools. Wand dueling and dance sessions to "Dance Like a Beauxbatons" and "Battle Like a Durmstrang" were also available. The usual question-and-answer panel was held along with a wand-raising tribute to Alan Rickman.

The fourth annual A Celebration of Harry Potter was held from January 27 to 29, 2017. The actors appearing for this event included Tom Felton (Draco Malfoy), Jason Isaacs (Lucius Malfoy), Matthew Lewis (Neville Longbottom), and Warwick David (Flitwick and Griphook), all of whom were available for the question-and-answer session.

New to this event was a trivia test called Audible Recall designed by Pottermore that they claim "will really sort the Hermiones from the Crabbes and Goyles." Warner Bros. Interactive Entertainment presented a virtual reality experience of *Fantastic Beasts and Where to Find Them* narrated by Newt Scamander. Production props imagery from the West End stage show *Harry Potter and the Cursed Child* and props from the production were on display. Designers Eduardo Lima and Miraphora Mina of MinaLima presented several iconic pieces of their work, including Hogwarts school books, back issues of *The Daily Prophet*, and the Marauders' Map. Warner Bros. Studio Tour Leavesden was there with a mini-tour experience, replete with costumes, props, and sets from the Harry Potter movies, and the curators of the Harry Potter:

The Exhibition offered interactive experiences such as the Sorting Hat and Quaffle Toss.

Other creative talent appeared as well with the return of Paul Harris, Nick Dudman, and Pierre Bohanna, and the addition of Mary GrandPre, illustrator of the early editions of the Scholastic Harry Potter books at a meet and greet. Warner Bros. Interactive Entertainment gave guests a chance to experience the Wizarding World in LEGO Dimensions and explore the worlds of Harry Potter and Fantastic Beasts.

Universal Studios Beijing

In October 2014, Tom Williams, Universal Parks and Resorts CEO, announced that Universal had signed a deal to build Universal Beijing, a $3.3 billion theme park resort property. The 1000-acre Beijing property was to include an assortment of rides and attractions in a 300-acre theme park. Many of these would be replicated from the other Universal theme parks as well as new attractions that reflect China's cultural heritage. Universal Studios Beijing will "pay proper homage to Chinese culture," said Williams. Outside the theme park there will be a Universal CityWalk retail and dining zone as well as a themed Universal resort hotel.

Comcast NBCUniversal is building the new Beijing theme park resort with four Chinese state-owned partners. Unlike Osaka and Singapore, which were built in a franchise style with local owners, this Universal Studios park will be the first foreign-owned theme park in the Chinese capital. The property is located in the eastern Beijing suburb of Tongzhou and was reportedly purchased in a deal made the previous March. Tongzhou is known as an area to which some of Beijing's city government is in the process of moving, to alleviate traffic congestion and pollution in the city center.

While no attractions were named when the official announcement was made, it was speculated that they would be based on the films most popular in China, including *Transformers*, *Despicable Me*, and Harry Potter.

When concept artwork of the park was later released, sharp eyes identified areas that could be identified as Transformers,

Revenge of the Mummy, Shrek, and Harry Potter. The latter appeared to be Hogwarts Castle, Hogsmeade Village, Diagon Alley, Escape from Gringotts, King's Cross Station, and Flight of the Hippogriff.

An official signing ceremony was held in September 2015 in New York at Comcast's headquarters with Comcast signing an agreement with the China consortium Shouhuan Beijing Cultural Tourism Investment Co. Ltd. to build Universal Studios Beijing. "Famous Hollywood director Steven Spielberg will be involved in the design of the park which will include many Chinese elements," Xinhua News Agency reported. Plans for a second theme park, a water park, and as many as five hotels were also unveiled for the site. Local newspapers reported construction could begin before the end of 2015 with a 2019 completion date.

By 2016 extensive land clearing was underway at the Tongzhou site. Several buildings had been removed or were being demolished and a small river running through the property was being diverted. The initial $3.3 billion theme park announced in 2014 has now secured $7.4 (US) billion in investment, Xinhua News reported. At a ground-breaking ceremony, it was announced that the opening date had been pushed back to 2020.

There does not seem to be an end in sight to people's fascination with the magical world of Harry Potter and it will now be left to subsequent editions of *Wizarding Worlds* to tell the rest of the story behind the Universal theme parks around the world.

BIBLIOGRAPHY

Books

Anelli, Melissa. *Harry, A History*. Pocket Books, 2008.

Budge, Zygmunt (J. K. Rowling). *Wonderbook: Book of Potions*.

Eisner, Michael. *Work in Progress*. Hyperion, 1998.

Fraser, Lindsey. *Conversations with J. K. Rowling*. Scholastic, 2001.

Gennaway, Sam. *JayBangs: How Jay Stein, MCA, and Universal Invented the Modern Theme Park and Beat Disney at Its Own Game*. Theme Park Press, 2016.

Green, Jerry. *25 Years Inside Universal Studios: From Tour Guide to Entertainment Director*. Theme Park Press, 2017.

Kubersky, Seth. *Disneyland 2017*. AdventureKeen, 2017.

Kubersky, Seth. *The Unofficial Guide to Universal Orlando 2017*. AdventureKeen, 2017.

Kurtti, Jeff. *Since the World Began: Walt Disney World the First 25 Years*. Hyperion, 1996.

McCabe, Bob. *Harry Potter: Page to Screen*. Harper Design, 2011.

Neal, Julie and Mike. *The Complete Universal Orlando: The Definitive Universal Handbook*. Coconut Press, 2016.

Niles, Robert. *Theme Park Insider visits the Wizarding World of Harry Potter*. Niles Online, 2016.

Peerless, Grant and Riding, Richard. *Leavesden Aerodrome: From Halifaxes to Hogwarts*. Amberley Publishing, 2011.

Revenson, Jody. *Harry Potter: Magical Places from the Films*. Harper Collins, 2015.

Revenson, Jody. *Harry Potter: The Artifact Vault*. Harper Collins, 2016.

Revenson, Jody. *Harry Potter: The Character Vault*. Harper Collins, 2015.

Revenson, Jody. *Harry Potter: The Creature Vault*. Harper Collins, 2014.

Rowling, J. K. *Harry Potter and the Chamber of Secrets*. Raincoast Books, 1999.

Rowling, J. K. *Harry Potter and the Deathly Hallows*. Raincoast Books, 2007.

Rowling, J. K. *Harry Potter and the Goblet of Fire*. Raincoast Books, 2000.

Rowling, J. K. *Harry Potter and the Half-Blood Prince*. Raincoast Books, 2005.

Rowling, J. K. *Harry Potter and the Order of the Phoenix*. Raincoast Books, 2003.

Rowling, J. K. *Harry Potter and the Philosopher's Stone*. Raincoast Books, 1999.

Rowling, J. K. *Harry Potter and the Prisoner of Azkaban*. Raincoast Books, 1999.

Rowling, J. K. *Fantastic Beasts and Where to Find Them: The Original Screenplay*. Scholastic, 2016.

Salisbury, Mark. *The Case of Beasts: Explore the Film Wizardry of Fantastic Beasts and Where to Find Them*. Harper Collins, 2016.

Scamander, Newt (J. K. Rowling). *Fantastic Beasts and Where to Find Them*. Pottermore, 2016.

Shapiro, Marc. *J. K. Rowling: The Wizard Behind Harry Potter*. St. Martin's Griffin, 2007.

Sibley, Brian. *Harry Potter Film Wizardry*. Harper Collins, 2010.

Silvester, William. *Harry Potter Collector's Handbook*. Krause Publications, 2010.

Sim, Nick. *Universal Orlando: The Unofficial Story*. CreateSpace, 2014.

Smith, Sean. *J. K. Rowling: A Biography: The Genius Behind Harry Potter*. Arrow, 2002.

Whisp, Kennilworthy (J. K. Rowling). *Quidditch Through the Ages*. Arthur A. Levine Books, 2017.

Studio Guides

The Making of Harry Potter: The Official Guide. Warner Bros. Studio Tour London.

The Wizarding World of Harry Potter. Universal Studios Hollywood.

The Wizarding World of Harry Potter. Universal Studios Japan.

The Wizarding World of Harry Potter. Universal Studios Orlando.

DVDs

Harry Potter and the Chamber of Secrets. ("Tour Diagon Alley").

Harry Potter and the Half-Blood Prince ("Get a Sneak Peek at Wizarding World of Harry Potter").

Websites

http://attractionsmagazine.com

http://bailiffgatemuseum.co.uk

http://www.eatyourkimchi.com

http://www.ges.com

https://www.harrypotterplatform934.com

http://harrypotter.wikia.com

http://www.hollywoodreporter.com

http://www.imdb.com

http://www.japantimes.co.jp

http://jimhillmedia.com

http://www.latimes.com

http://www.leaderpost.com

http://www.the-leaky-cauldron.org

http://magical-menagerie.com

http://www.miaminewtimes.com

http://www.moviesculptor.com

http://www.mugglenet.com

http://www.nationalledger.com

http://www.northumberlandgazette.co.uk

http://www.orlandosentinel.com

https://parkpedia.wordpress.com

https://www.parkz.com.au

http://www.thepassportlifestyle.com

http://www.popularmechanics.com/culture/movies

https://www.pottermore.com

http://www.rappler.com

http://www.screamscape.com

http://www.slashfilm.com

https://www.snitchseeker.com

http://www.telegraph.co.uk

http://www.themeparkinsider.com

http://www.themeparktourist.com

http://www.traveling-up.com

https://touringplans.com

https://universalstudioshollywood.com

https://www.wbstudiotour.co.uk

https://www.wbstudiotour.com/harry-potter-fantastic-beasts

https://ww2.universalorlando.com

https://www.usj.co.jp

http://www.visitorlando.com

http://wizardsandwhatnot.com

http://web.archive.org

http://www.yesterland.com

ABOUT THE AUTHOR

Bill Silvester is a prolific author, with hundreds of articles, mostly historical in nature, to his name.

As a philatelist, he began writing about Disney postage stamps, a previously unfilled niche in Disneyana. This resulted in numerous articles in philatelic publications and a bi-monthly newsletter. In the 1990s, his *Handbook of Disney Philately* was published, followed by *Harry Potter Collector's Handbook in 2010* and *A Solo Wargamer's Guide* in 2013. In 2012, the American Topical Association published his *Handbook of Disney on Stamps* with full-color illustrations of all the Disney stamps issued from 1968 to date and the stories behind them.

For Theme Park Press, he is the author of two previous books: *The Adventures of Young Walt Disney* (2014) and *Saving Disney* (2015), a biography of Roy E. Disney.

For more, visit williamsilvester.weebly.com.

ABOUT THEME PARK PRESS

Theme Park Press publishes books primarily about the Disney company, its history, culture, films, animation, and theme parks, as well as theme parks in general.

Our authors include noted historians, animators, Imagineers, and experts in the theme park industry.

We also publish many books by first-time authors, with topics ranging from fiction to theme park guides.

And we're always looking for new talent. If you'd like to write for us, or if you're interested in the many other titles in our catalog, please visit:

www.ThemeParkPress.com

Theme Park Press Newsletter

Subscribe to our free email newsletter and enjoy:

- Free book downloads and giveaways
- Access to excerpts from our many books
- Announcements of forthcoming releases
- Exclusive additional content and chapters
- And more good stuff available nowhere else

To subscribe, visit www.ThemeParkPress.com, or send email to newsletter@themeparkpress.com.

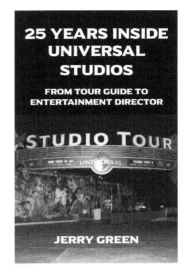

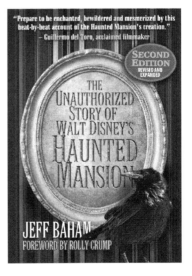

Read more about these books and our many other titles at:

www.ThemeParkPress.com

Made in the USA
Columbia, SC
06 December 2017